DIVERSE PATHWAYS

T0288246

Ruth Simms Hamilton
AFRICAN DIASPORA SERIES

DIVERSE PATHWAYS: RACE AND THE INCORPORATION OF BLACK, WHITE, AND ARAB-ORIGIN AFRICANS IN THE UNITED STATES

Kevin J. A. Thomas

MICHIGAN STATE UNIVERSITY PRESS • *East Lansing*

∞ The paper used in this publication meets the minimum requirements of
ANSI/NISO Z39.48-1992 (R 1997) (Permanence of Paper).

Michigan State University Press
East Lansing, Michigan 48823-5245

Printed and bound in the United States of America.

20   19   18   17   16   15   14   1   2   3   4   5   6   7   8   9   10

LIBRARY OF CONGRESS CATALOGING-IN-PUBLICATION DATA
Thomas, Kevin J. A.
Diverse pathways : race and the incorporation of Black, White, and Arab-origin
Africans in the United States / Kevin J. A. Thomas.
pages cm.—(African diaspora series)
Includes bibliographical references and index.
ISBN 978-1-61186-104-4 (pbk. : alk. paper)—ISBN 978-1-60917-395-1 (ebook)
1. Africans—Cultural assimilation—United States. 2. Africans—United
States—Social conditions. 3. Africans—United States—Economic conditions.
4. Immigrants—United States—Social conditions. 5. Immigrants—United
States—Economic conditions. 6. Africa—Emigration and immigration—Social
aspects. 7. United States—Emigration and immigration—Social aspects. 8.
United States—Race relations. 9. Social surveys—United States. I. Title.
E184.A24T46 2014
973'.0496—dc23
2013014958

Book design by Charlie Sharp, Sharp Des!gns, Lansing, Michigan
Cover design by Erin Kirk New
Cover art ©iStockphoto.com/ Pesky Monkey

Michigan State University Press is a member of the Green Press Initiative and is committed
to developing and encouraging ecologically responsible publishing practices. For more
information about the Green Press Initiative and the use of recycled paper in book publishing,
please visit www.greenpressinitiative.org.

Visit Michigan State University Press at www.msupress.org

Contents

Acknowledgments

When I was a student in graduate school the thought of writing a book hardly ever crossed my mind. After my advisor suggested that I seriously consider writing a book, I developed a greater appreciation for the role books play in advancing scholarly discourses. It was several years later that I started the process of writing one. Given my research interest in African immigrants, it seemed logical for me to start with a book on this population, paying attention to the examination of their outcomes from a nuanced perspective. In the end, I chose an angle that interrogates the influence of race and Arab ethnicity on their incorporation process. Little did I know that in order to convert these ideas into a manuscript, I would need the assistance of a wide range of individuals and institutions. I thank God that these resources were eventually aligned in a way that allowed me to initiate and complete this project on race and African immigration.

The development of my ideas invariably relied on the knowledge and insights of mentors and colleagues. Now more than ever, I better appreciate my graduate training in international migration because it provided an important foundation for the analysis presented in this book. My key mentors included Tukufu Zuberi and Francis Dodoo. Dodoo is a leading scholar on the African Diaspora in the United States and a senior colleague with whom I had very frequent scholarly interactions. His work on African immigrants in the United States provided a useful resource that informed my thoughts on how best to extend the analysis of the immigrants' social and economic outcomes. I am also grateful for the mentoring I received from John Iceland. John has published a number of books, and his invaluable insights helped me understand the basics of the publishing process including developing a book proposal.

More generally, my work on African immigrants has benefited from the mentoring of senior professors and colleagues including Gordon De Jong, Hans-Peter Kohler, Nancy Landale, Ikubolajeh Logan, Douglas Massey, Sal Oropesa, Emilie Smith, Jennifer Van Hook, and Keith Wilson. I am also grateful for the support provided by the immigration interest group at the Population Research Institute at Pennsylvania State University. Similar types of support were provided by Pennsylvania State University's Center for Family Research in Diverse Contexts. Colleagues in the Department of African and African American Studies and the Africana Research Center also provided useful feedback that was crucial to the development of the book. Indeed, some of the ideas in this book were presented at the Africana Research Center's brown bag seminar during which I received insightful comments from other researchers.

During the writing and review processes, I quickly realized how blessed I was to have several sources of support through what can sometimes be an arduous routine. Tina Thomas, my wife, deserves special acknowledgment. She demonstrated tremendous patience while I was occupied with the writing process, and was gracious enough to be a sounding board for my ideas. I am also grateful for her willingness to read, and sometimes edit, the manuscript. Jeremiah and Floretta Thomas provided their usual words of encouragement—the kind of uplifting words good parents typically give to their children. During the review process, I developed a great level of appreciation for the assistance provided by series editor Kimberly Simmons and by Julie Loehr of the Michigan State University Press. Their guidance in navigating the vicissitudes of the review process was very instrumental in the development of the final version of the manuscript. For all their support during this process I would like to say thanks.

Race, Ethnicity, and African Immigration to the United States

History was made when the winner of the Oscar for best actress was announced in 2004. Before then, no African had won the coveted Oscar for best actress at the Academy Awards ceremony. Given the limited number of African actors in Hollywood, the chances of having an African-born Oscar winner were indeed very small. For her performance in the movie *Monster*, however, Charlize Theron won the Oscar for best actress in 2004 and was able to do what no African had done before. Interestingly, though, as she celebrated with her colleagues that evening, equally illustrious celebrations were being planned on the other side of the Atlantic. A few weeks later, Theron traveled to her native South Africa, where the celebrations continued. These celebrations included events in which she was the special guest of fellow South African native Nelson Mandela and then South African president Thabo Mbeki (Silverman 2004).

Theron's story exemplifies the hopes of many Africans who desire to migrate to the United States. Declining living standards and the possibilities for advancement provide the right mix of circumstances driving recent increases in African migration to the United States. Africans are not unique in their desire to pursue higher living standards in the United States. As the world's leading country of immigration, the United States traditionally attracts migrants from the major world regions. In an international survey conducted by the Gallup Organization between 2007 and 2009, the United States was found to be the most desired destination of potential migrants among respondents in 135 countries (Esipova and Ray 2009). Tellingly, the greatest desire to migrate to the United States was found among respondents in sub-Saharan Africa. In recent decades, African nationals have increasingly been able to translate these desires into actual migration decisions. Consequently, in the last thirty years, significant increases have occurred in the size of America's African-born population. Towards the end of the previous century, for example, Africans were among the fastest-growing immigrant groups in the United States (Rumbaut 1994). These trends suggest that contemporary African migration flows have profound implications for understanding how recent immigrant groups are incorporated into US society.

In many ways, Charlize Theron, who is White, represents the complexities involved in describing the new face of African immigrants living in the United States. Compared to the racial homogeneity that characterized America's African-born population for much of the past four centuries, contemporary African immigrants are more racially diverse. Like Theron, many of them are racially White. Yet, as in previous centuries, Black Africans continue to feature prominently in the dynamics of contemporary African migration to the United States. Recent waves of African immigrants also include people of Arab ethnic origins, who mainly come from northern and eastern Africa and have social and cultural attributes that are distinct from those of non-Arab Africans. Arab immigration from African countries has also contributed to the increased growth and transformation of the Arab American population. According to US census estimates, the total Arab-origin population of the United States increased by about 40 percent between 1990 and 2000; this growth was partly driven by an 82 percent increase in Arab immigration from Egypt, in North Africa, during this period (De la Cruz and Brittingham 2003).

Notwithstanding this increase, Arab immigrants are particularly overlooked in the scholarly discourse on African immigration to the United States or the African Diaspora in general. As a result, little is known concerning whether there are variations in incorporation processes of Africans of Arab and non-Arab ethnic origins. Hochschild and Cropper (2010) use the term *incorporation* to describe the process by which immigrants are absorbed or merged into the larger US society and become better able to engage in its activities. In this book, this definition is employed with several caveats in mind. Heisler (1992) suggests, for example, that the process fails to capture the realities of domestic minorities such as Native Americans and African Americans, whose colonization experiences have exposed them to a long history of systematic exclusion from society. Thus, she argues, despite recent improvements in their welfare, they have not been fully integrated into society based on traditional notions of incorporation. Based on the work of Portes and Borocz (1989), the process should also be considered as a general derivation of the functionalist paradigm in sociology that is typically applied to foreign minorities. Essentially, the dynamics of incorporation do not precisely capture the experiences of domestic minorities; they are more useful for examining the social realities of immigrant groups. It is in this sense that the incorporation processes of Arab and non-Arab Africans into US society are examined here.

Complicating the analysis of Arab incorporation, however, are the peculiar and diverse racial characteristics of Arab immigrants. Although there is a lack of consensus on how to racially classify Arabs, the US census indicates that about 80 percent of Arabs identify themselves as White (De la Cruz and Brittingham 2003). A smaller proportion of Arabs identify themselves as Black or as members of other racial groups. Despite these racial variations, however, the implications of Arab racial diversity for understanding African immigrant incorporation processes have not been systematically examined. Furthermore, although most Arabs identify themselves as White, similarities and differences in incorporation between White Arab immigrants and White immigrants of non-Arab origins have not been extensively investigated.

Other differences found among African immigrants in the United States relate to their degree of social and economic achievement. One picture of African immigrants featured in American popular culture is that related to their successes. Like Theron, for example, sports star Hakeem Olajuwon, a member of the Basketball Hall of Fame, and Arab American, Nobel Prize–winning professor Ahmed Zewail, are also African natives. Americans have also become familiar with another successful African who immigrated to the United States in the late 1950s: Harvard-educated economist Barack Obama Sr., father of President Barack Obama.

For many other African immigrants, in contrast, success has been elusive. Refugees from conflicts in Africa as well as African immigrants in poor inner-city neighborhoods face some of the most severe constraints on social mobility (A. Hughes 2006). In some cases, poverty rates among these groups exceed the US national average (Wilson 2008). Significantly, however, the studies examining the welfare of disadvantaged African immigrant groups generally suggest that these socioeconomic constraints are more likely to be concentrated among Black than non-Black Africans (A. Hughes 2006; Wilson 2008). Furthermore, African immigrants, especially those who are Black, experience issues related to racism, discrimination, and other indicators of disadvantage that characterize the lives of US-born Blacks (Arthur 2000; Portes and Zhou 1992). Apart from the fact that these limitations have negatively affected the social mobility of Black Africans in Western societies, they also have negative implications for their health and psychological adjustment, as has been observed among US-born Black populations (Danso and Grant 2000; Gee and Laflamme 2006).

Overall, disparities in social and economic achievement among African immigrants, especially those defined by race, suggest that there is considerable variation in their prospects for social and economic mobility. However, studies documenting these differences or investigating systematic differences in African immigrants' pathways of incorporation are generally lacking. As a result it has been difficult to make definitive statements concerning whether these disparities are a product of variations in the opportunities available to African immigrant subgroups. Similarly, in the absence of such studies, little is known concerning how attributes such as ethnicity and human capital influence the types of resources available to Africans as they assimilate into society.

In this book, therefore, the underlying basis for understanding the socioeconomic mobility patterns of African immigrants in the United States is a sociological analysis of the ways in which race and ethnic characteristics influence their incorporation processes. Accordingly, a major argument presented in the analysis is that racial and ethnic differences among African immigrants are important for understanding the constraints and opportunities available to them as they assimilate into US society. When possible, this argument is reinforced using empirical evidence using recent data from the American Community Survey (ACS). These data are particularly useful because they contain information respondents' self-identified race and ethnic ancestry.

Consistent with research underscoring the fact that African immigrants are recent immigrants (Thomas 2011a), the overwhelming majority of immigrants in the study (96 percent) arrived after the 1965 immigration reforms. In fact, their median year of arrival is 1997. One implication of these patterns is the fact that most of the African Arabs immigrants found in the analysis arrived before the events of September 11, 2001. On average, their incorporation process started before these events, but these processes still occurred within a pre–September 11, 2001, context in which an Arab identity was associated with social inequalities. At the same time, it is not unreasonable to expect the post–September 11, 2001, racial context to have had additional negative implications for their patterns of social mobility. Consequently, the effects of these more recent influences are not necessarily discounted.

In general, however, the book's central arguments are presented from a number of critical viewpoints. For example, perspectives on racial and ethnic minority disadvantage in both Africa and the United States are used as foundational bases for understanding why African racial and ethnic differences are likely to influence the types of barriers and opportunities available to them. A major portion of the book also highlights racial and ethnic inequalities in specific outcomes relevant for understanding variations in the social and economic attainment of Africans. We examine, for example, whether Black Africans experience patterns of occupational incorporation similar to those of White African immigrants. The consequences of these differences for economic indicators such as earnings are also assessed. The book also investigates educational attainment patterns across race and examines variations in marital incorporation in order to make inferences about disparities in the disappearance of cultural barriers between Africans and US natives.

By focusing on these issues we expect to identify key differences in the possibilities for social mobility available to African immigrant subgroups. In the process, the analysis contributes to the development of a nuanced portrait of African immigrant experiences. More importantly, the issues examined in this book have profound implications for our overall understanding of how African immigrants are becoming American. In other words, among African immigrants, racial and ethnic inequalities provide a unique understanding of the essential question of what it means to become an American of African origin. Answers to this question will vary considerably depending on factors such as skin color and human-capital differences. Beyond these issues, the analysis is also important for illuminating the dynamics of broader disparities within US society. For example, it will demonstrate how the disparities observed among African immigrants reinforce patterns of racial inequality found in the overall US population.

AFRICAN MIGRATION IN INTERNATIONAL PERSPECTIVE

The historical and contemporary dimensions of African migration provide an important contextual basis for understanding the recent surge in African immigration to the United States. Africans, in general, have always been migratory. A number of studies indicate that the oldest evidence of migration among modern humans is found in Africa (Osborne et al. 2008; Quintana-Murci et al. 1999). Migration, as a social process, therefore, has its origins within African societies. Historically, Africa has also served as an origin country of immigrants to what is now the United States for much longer than most other regions of the world. Evidence suggests that the first enslaved Africans arrived at the San

Miguel de Gualdape colony, in what is now the United States, in 1526 (Pickett and Pickett 2011). Another set of Black Africans is also believed to have arrived in the United States about a year before the pilgrims reached Plymouth Rock in 1620 (Kollehlon and Eule 2003). For the next two and a half centuries, Africans dominated migration movements at the global level, as more than ten million slaves were forcibly transported from Africa to the United States and the New World. This first wave of mass migration from Africa to the United States generally ended after slavery was declared illegal in 1808. Subsequently, Africa was replaced by Europe as the most important source of migrants across the globe; European domination of world migration continued for much of the nineteenth century and into the first two decades of the twentieth century (Massey 1990).

At the end of European domination of world migration flows, Africa and other developing countries again emerged as major sources of international migration movements. Estimates for the period between 1965 and 1990, for example, indicate that Africa experienced larger increases in international migrants than other world regions during this period (Zlotnik 1998). These increases were driven by declining economic fortunes, political instability, and social and demographic transitions in African countries in the postindependence era (Hatton and Williamson 2003). By the second half of the twentieth century, the United States had once again become the leading destination country for Africans migrating to more industrialized countries.

Apart from the United States, developed countries in Europe, South America, and other regions also became attractions to African nationals migrating after the 1960s. At the start of the twenty-first century, for example, Africans accounted for at least 10 percent of the foreign-born population of Finland, Denmark, Netherlands, and Iceland (Salt 2005). Likewise, in Canada, the African-born population experienced a fifty-fold increase between the late 1950s and the end of the twentieth century (Konadu-Agyemang and Takyi 2006). Beyond Europe and North America, however, Asia, South America, and the Middle East have also become important destinations for African international migrants (Adepoju 1991; Massey et al. 1998). Among the consequences of this new wave of African international migration is the emergence of new African Diaspora populations in an increasing number of countries across the globe. Most of these countries were previously considered to be nontraditional destinations for African migrants.

With regard to the US experience, the recent growth in its African-born population is somewhat similar to what was observed during the early period of the slave trade. More generally, the growth patterns seen among recent African immigrants are unprecedented on three important dimensions. First, they represent the first large-scale arrival of voluntary African migrants in the history of the United States. In fact, some estimates indicate that since 1990 the number of African immigrants arriving in the United States has exceeded the total number of Africans who arrived during the period of slavery (Roberts 2005). Second, contemporary African immigrants to the United States are more diverse in terms of their racial, social, and cultural characteristics. In contrast to African migration during the period of slavery, which involved exclusively Black African populations, recent African immigrants include Blacks, Whites, and even a small number of African-born Asians. These Asians are primarily from countries such as Uganda, Kenya, and South Africa that attracted migrants from Asia for significant periods in their history.

A third peculiar dimension of the new wave of African immigration is related to the systematic increases in its size, especially during the last two decades. These increases have contributed to significant growth in the Black population of the United States and are also unprecedented in the last one and a half centuries. Between 2000 and 2005, for example, the annual number of African arrivals in the United States was close to 60,000 (Kent 2007). Put in perspective, this number exceeds the estimated 460 African immigrants who arrived in the United States annually between the years 1861 and 1961 (Konadu-Agyemang and Takyi 2006). Kent (2007) also indicates that of the total number of Africans living in the United States in 2005, approximately 1 million arrived after 1980, while only about 60,000 combined arrived in all years before then. Furthermore, according to Terrazas (2009), 1.4 million African immigrants lived in the United States in 2007; this is approximately forty times higher than the 35,000 number of Africans who lived in the United States in 1960. Trends in African immigrant arrivals between 1982 and 1998 also underscore the notion that systematically greater numbers of African immigrants arrived in the United States in the years leading up to the end of the twentieth century. Accordingly, although about 200,000 Africans arrived between 1982 and 1992, a similar number arrived in the United States in the four-year period between 1995 and 1998 (Konadu-Agyemang and Takyi 2006).

RACIAL DIFFERENCES AMONG AFRICANS

Discourses on the conceptualization of race in African societies provide an essential backdrop for understanding racial differences among Africans as well as their implications. Without doubt, Africa is the home of the majority of the world's Black population. However, the continent also has a sizable population of non-Black natives. The racial diversity that characterizes African societies has, therefore, been the focus of scholarly research for more than half a century. Criteria used to identify African racial differences vary, ranging from the use of physical characteristics to an emphasis on a combination of physical and social characteristics in classification systems used to achieve larger social and political objectives.

Early work by Seligman (1966) used characteristics such as skin color, hair form, head shape, and stature to distinguish between what he considered to be the five principle races in Africa. These races were the Hamites, Semites, Negros, Khosians, and Negrillos. This taxonomy has, however, been criticized for, among other things, being seemingly based on stereotypes (Keita and Kittles 1997). Yet, in recent decades, another racial classification system has been observed by scholars working on Sudan. These systems are embedded within Sudanese linguistic descriptions of racial groups and have historically involved the use of a wider range of colors. Accordingly, colors such as "blue" and "green" were used to describe generally Black Sudanese populations, depending on, among other things, their social class and skin tone (Bender 1983; Sharkey 2007). An even more recent and more well-known racial classification system was developed in South Africa, where racial definitions used during apartheid were based on skin color differences and were used to achieve specific social objectives (Dubow 1992). In this context, the term "White" was generally used to identify White South Africans of European descent, the most privileged racial group, while "honorary white" was used to described some non-White groups such as the Japanese that distinctively lacked a Black skin tone (Osada 2002). This distinction made it possible for "honorary whites" to receive a number of privileges that were not extended to the South African Black population, who were at the bottom of the racial stratification system.

To the extent that race is socially constructed and associated with differences in skin color, African immigrants, upon arrival in the United States, are classified into two major groups; Black and White. This dichotomy has two important implications. First, the US racial classification system understates the true racial diversity found among Africans in the United States, at least with regard to how Africans choose to identify themselves. In Chacko's (2003) study among Ethiopians, for example, all respondents interviewed identified themselves as "Black," using the US racial classification system. Yet the majority of them expressed a preference for "African" as their ideal racial marker of choice. A second implication arising from the Black-White racial dichotomy is that because US constructions of race fail to recognize their peculiar manifestations in African societies, the pre- and postimmigration racial identities of many African immigrants are likely to differ. South Africans of mixed-race origin are illustrative of this point. While lighter-skinned Blacks, with both Black and White South African ancestry, are likely to be classified as "Colored" in their country of origin, upon their arrival in the United States they are more likely to be considered to be Black than White or Colored.

Notwithstanding these limitations, however, the book focuses on the general Black-White racial dichotomy found among Africans. One advantage of using this approach is that it reflects the analytical strategy used in research on racial stratification in the United States that focus on Blacks and Whites, the groups found at polar ends of the socioeconomic spectrum. There are, however, other reasons for focusing on the Black-White racial dichotomy among Africans. First, these two groups account for the majority of African immigrants living in the United States. In combination, they represented slightly more than 93 percent of the African-born population in the United States according to estimates from the 2000 US census. Second, the book argues that US conceptualizations of race influences African immigrant incorporation processes, precisely because, American, not African, racial differences affect their access to social and economic opportunities. Previous studies (e.g., Gordon 1998) also underscore the fact that contemporary African migration to the United States is generally dominated by Black and White Africans. Studies on African immigration, therefore, tend to focus on either one these two groups, especially on the outcomes of the former. Given the lack of research on White African immigrants, however, little is known about their origins, patterns of immigration, and their degree of integration into the broader US society.

White Africans

White African natives are an essential part of the African population, although their influence in African societies has been on a decline. In general, their origins can be traced to the long history of European contact with traditional African societies. Chege (1997), for example, traces the presence of White Europeans in Africa as far back as the days of the Roman general Mark Antony, who was married to Cleopatra, the queen of Egypt. The systematic involvement of predominantly White European nation-states in Africa can, however, be traced to the period of the first post-Roman European incursion into Africa around 1415 (L'Ange 2005). Nevertheless, it was the start of European colonization efforts in Africa towards the end of the nineteenth century that resulted in an unprecedented level of migration of White populations from Europe to Africa. These migrants mainly came from five countries: Portugal, England, the Netherlands, France, and Germany (Hammer 2010; L'Ange 2005), and their settlement in Africa was aided by the discovery of quinine, which reduced deaths from malaria, and by missionary efforts to expand Christianity (West 1965).

As European colonial powers consolidated their administrations in Africa, White settlements around the continent increased even more dramatically. Most of the initial increase was concentrated in northern and southern African countries. However, much later in the colonial period, similar increases were observed in eastern Africa as new White settlements were created in countries such as Kenya, Uganda, and Tanzania (West 1965). A second wave of White European immigration to Africa occurred after the end of the Second World War. This wave involved the arrival of more than 300,000 Whites in the first seven postwar years, and was in absolute terms the largest inflow of White populations into Africa (L'Ange 2005). Europeans migrating to Africa during this period were largely doing so to escape declining economic conditions in postwar Europe.

Towards the end of the 1950s, as many countries gained their independence, Africa began to lose its appeal to White European immigrants. Furthermore, increasing violence during the independence struggle in some countries, and the limited need for European bureaucrats in newly independent African states, also contributed to increased rates of White African out-migration to Europe (Chege 1997). A few White Africans, however, chose to remain and continued to maintain many of the economic privileges enjoyed by White Europeans in Africa during the colonial period.

Still another period of White out-migration from Africa occurred towards the end of the twentieth century. Most of these migrants were from South Africa and left at the end of apartheid as a result of growing fears of social and political turmoil (Kabwe-Segatti et al. 2006; Johnson 2009). Hammer (2010), however, estimates there are about seven million White natives living in Africa, the majority of whom can be found in South Africa, although White Africans can still be found in parts of eastern and northern Africa. Hammer's estimate, however, suggests that White Africans account for less than 1 percent of the total African population. As a result of high levels of White African emigration to the United States in the second half of the previous century, US census data indicates that White Africans accounted for about 30 percent of the African-born population of the United States in the year 2000.

African Arabs

African Arabs largely trace their ancestral origins to the Arabian Peninsula and are a product of interactions between African and Middle Eastern societies over a span about twelve centuries. As early as the seventh century much of North Africa was controlled by Arab Muslim conquerors (Boone and Benco 1999). In the ensuing centuries, interactions between African societies and those in the Arabian Peninsula were mainly for purposes of commerce. A major part of these activities revolved around the trade in slaves and the subsequent settlement of Arab slave traders in parts of Africa. According to Grandmaison (1989), for example, Al-Harty Arab traders from Oman were involved in the slave trade in Ethiopia as early as the tenth century, and were possibly the first foreign immigrants to settle in eastern African society. As a result of high levels of Arab settlement in Africa over time, the continent now accounts for a significant proportion of the world's Arab population. In fact, Egypt, which has the world's largest Arab population, is located in North Africa, while approximately half of the member states of the Arab League are found within the African continent.

Like other Arab populations, African Arabs are characterized by important patterns of racial disparity (Al-Khatib 2006). In terms of skin color, Arabs can generally be classified into three broad groups (El-Essawi et al. 2007; Mazuri 1964). These include White Arabs, found in much of the Arab world; Brown or olive-skinned Arabs, such as those found in Yemen; and Black Arabs who live in parts of Africa, Oman, and Saudi Arabia. Black Arab Africans emerged in North Africa and the Middle East as an increasing number of Black slaves were transported from sub-Saharan Africa by Arab slave-traders during the trans-Saharan slave trade (Segal 2002). Furthermore, historical evidence suggests that Black Arab populations in other parts of Africa were a product of sexual relationships between Arab traders and African females, especially in areas such as Zanzibar and Sudan (Mazuri 1973; Segal 2002).

Despite recent growth of African immigration to the United States, knowledge on the extent to which the interaction between race and Arab ethnicity influences the outcomes for African immigrants is generally limited. Arab African immigrants specifically differ from non-Arab Africans in ways that have important implications for their incorporation into US society. Arab Africans, for example, largely originate from premigration contexts in which the predominant language spoken is Arabic. African immigrants from these contexts have lower levels of English proficiency than Africans from English-speaking countries (Thomas 2010). Language differences may thus result in important differences in acculturation between White Arab Africans and their non-Arab counterparts, who mainly come from English-speaking African societies.

Another unique characteristic of Arab African immigrants is the fact that they originate from predominantly Islamic societies. Accordingly, Arab African immigrants, more than their non-Arab counterparts, are likely to have religious practices that differ from those practiced by the majority of the US population. The question of whether or not these practices, or the stereotypes associated with them, facilitate or impede the incorporation processes of African immigrants has not been examined in previous studies. What seems clear is that the lived experiences of African Arabs are unfolding within a period characterized by increased levels of "Islamophobia." As Shryock (2010) maintains, Islamophobia, or the generalized fear of Islam and Muslims, is responsible for acts of mosque vandalism and the perpetration of hate crimes against individuals perceived to be Muslim. In addition, Bayoumi (2008) surmises that Arab Americans are now the new problem group in the United States. He argues that Arabs and Muslims live in what he considers to be the first new communities of suspicion in the post-civil rights era. Under these circumstances, it is not clear that the conceptual advantage associated with Whiteness will be as pronounced among White Arabs as it is among non-Arab Whites. Differences in incorporation between Arab and non-Arab Blacks have also not been systematically examined in previous studies. However, broad cultural differences between these two groups may have significant implications for their respective patterns of social incorporation.

Racial differences among Arab Africans further raise critical questions concerning whether the postimmigration experiences of all Arab Africans are similar. Important insights are therefore likely to emerge from an analysis of the outcomes of Black and White Arab Africans as they become more integrated into US society. If, for example, socioeconomic inequalities are found between the two, they would suggest that racial minority status has important implications for understanding incorporation processes even among groups exposed to similar stereotypes associated with their broad ethnic characteristics.

RACE AND THE EVOLUTION OF AFRICAN IMMIGRATION TO THE UNITED STATES

Since the early origins of American society, conceptions of race have had important ramifications for understanding the dynamics of African immigration and settlement. For more than a century following the arrival of the first African slaves, the increasing significance of the slave trade, and the subsequent forced migration of Africans, was undergirded by a distinct ideology of Black racial inferiority. Scholars, however, disagree on whether or not this ideology was the principal cause of the transatlantic slave trade. In his classic work *White over Black*, for example, Jordan (1968) argues that European explorers' beliefs about the savagery and inferiority of Black Africans preceded their role in facilitating the forced migration of Africans during this period. Conversely, others suggest that the racial ideology associated with slavery was developed after the arrival of the first Black African slaves. According to this perspective, the racial ideology of slavery was developed to protect the economic interests of wealthy slaveowners who desired to protect their major source of cheap manual labor (Wilson 1996). At the height of the slave trade, however, ideological constructions based on the inferiority of Black Africans were widely used to justify the practice of enslavement. Despite the disagreement on the racial origins of slavery, however, it seems clear that the social context within which the immigration of African slaves occurred was at various points characterized by a systematic ideology of Black racial inferiority.

With the legal end of the US slave trade in 1808, the resulting decline in African immigration provided limited opportunities for observing how conceptions of race influenced migration between Africa and the United States. Yet, instructively the limited African immigration that occurred in the early part of the twentieth century was still a product of obvious racial influences on US immigration policy. In particular, the major strategy for immigration control during this period revolved around a series of exclusionary acts passed by Congress. Some commentators (e.g., Ngai 2009) suggest that these policies had significant racist undertones and were driven by a desire to restrict immigration flows deemed to be undesirable.

One such restriction was the National Origins Act of 1924. According to Daniels (2004), the act was preceded by a congressionally mandated study of the people in the United States in 1920. Beginning from 1929, the quota of immigrants permitted from each country reflected the percentage contribution of that immigrant group to the US population of 1920. Nevertheless, the definition of the US population used in the 1920 study explicitly excluded "descendants of slave immigrants," or people of African origin, who lived in the United States at that time (Daniels 2004, 55). As a result, the National Origins Act effectively eliminated all Black immigration to the United States until it was repealed in the mid-1960s. Fundamental to the political viability of such laws, DeLaet (2000) argues, was tolerance of the racism that was prevalent in the United States during this period. In general, these restrictions continued to have considerable impacts on racial and ethnic characteristics of immigrants in the first half the twentieth century. Among them is the fact that most immigrants to the United States during this period were non-Black, or more specifically White populations who were largely from western Europe (Portes and Zhou 1993).

As noted earlier, very limited African immigration occurred between the end of slavery and the first half of the twentieth century. Yet even these limited flows occurred along racial lines. For several decades following the end of slavery, for example, the limited number of African immigrants to the United States involved just a few Blacks from Cape Verde. These immigrants were allowed in the United States because their maritime skills were particularly prized by the US whaling industry for much of the 1800s (Wilson and Habecker 2008). For the most part, the African immigrants who arrived after this period were predominantly from two origin countries, Egypt and South Africa, the countries with the largest populations of White Africans of Arab and non-Arab origins respectively (Gordon 1998).

By the mid-1960s, the success of the civil rights movement had resulted in significant changes in perceptions of race within US society. Within this context, legislators believed that major changes were needed in US immigration policy in order to demonstrate America's entry into a new era of racial equality (Zolberg 1999). The Hart-Cellar Act, which was passed in 1965, thus removed the major restrictions that had constrained legal immigration from Africa and indeed, much of the developing world. In the debates leading up to the final vote on this legislation, subtle concerns were expressed about its presumed effect of once again increasing undesired immigration from Africa. According to Zolberg (1999), conservative legislators who were against the legislation, in an attempt to drum up fears of its expected consequences, argued that if passed, the Hart-Cellar Act would lead to a flood of African, as well as Asian, immigrants.

In the decades following the Hart-Cellar Act immigrants to the United States have increasingly come from more diverse origin countries, including those in Africa. Also resulting from these increases are important transformations in the racial and ethnic composition of the US population. For example, immigrants now account for at least a quarter of the growth of the US Black population (Logan and Deane 2003). Furthermore, as earlier noted, increases in Arab immigration from Egypt played an important role in the recent growth in the Arab population of the United States. Still, the surge in African migration after 1965 did not result in immediate changes in the racial composition of African immigrants in the United States. By the mid-1990s, for example, only about half of the African-born population of the United States was racially Black (Spear 1994). Nevertheless, consistent increases in Black immigration since 1990 have resulted in rapid shifts in the racial composition of Africans in the United States. As data from the 2006 to 2008 American Community Survey indicates, Black Africans now account for a little over 65 percent of all Africans living in the United States. In contrast, only about 28 percent of all African immigrants now identify themselves as White.

Even with the removal of origin country quotas in 1965, the influence of race still continues to have important implications for the dynamics of immigration from Africa. For example, the surge in contemporary migration from Africa to the United States started in the second half of the previous century in a period which, according to W. E. B Du Bois (1903), was to be defined by the problem of the color line. Thus, many new African immigrants arrived at a time when differences in skin color still had important implications for understanding differences in social and economic mobility. Lee and Bean (2004; 2010) more recently suggested that color lines are still relevant for understanding the social and demographic outcomes of Black populations in the twenty-first century. More poignantly, they suggest that the incorporation of recent immigrants is increasingly influenced by a new color line defined by a Black/non-Black divide. As more African immigrants arrive in the United States, therefore, their incorporation will continue to occur in a social context in which race strongly influences the dynamics of social mobility. In these circumstances, the US color line will have different implications for the welfare of Black and White Africans.

SUMMARY AND IMPLICATIONS

The growing number of African immigrants in the United States is part of a larger expansion of African international migration to new destinations in the West. In the United States, these increases are occurring within important political and social contexts. Immigration to the United States has traditionally been influenced by considerations of race while similar influences are known to affect prospects for social mobility. Notwithstanding these influences, our understanding of how African immigrants are incorporated into the United States is constrained by the tendency to conflate *African* with *Black*. In reality, Africans have diverse racial origins and are also differentiated by ethnic identity. Among the most important of these ethnic differences is that between Arab and non-Arab Africans, a distinction that is particularly important in post–September 11 US society.

Intersections between race and Arab ethnicity among Africans have important implications for understanding the dynamics of their incorporation into society. In part, these implications are theoretical. They pose important challenges to conventional theoretical perspectives used for understanding immigrant incorporation processes. One limitation is that some of these perspectives were developed using the experiences of non-African immigrants. Racial differences are also found within African origin countries; as such, they underscore the theoretical importance of premigration racial inequalities and their possible effects on social incorporation processes. Yet another theoretical implication of African racial and ethnic differences is associated with whether they result in similar inequalities as those found between US-born Blacks and Whites. If they do, they will underscore the persistent significance on race as a mediator of socioeconomic differences.

Other fundamental implications are associated with the extent to which racial and ethnic differences affect immigrants' attainment, as measured by specific types of indicators. In terms of education, for example, racial differences imply that the high levels of African immigrant achievement relative to the US-born found in previous studies requires further interrogation. If racial and ethnic minority statuses are important for understanding educational differences, then the presumption of Black African immigrants as model minorities is partly flawed. In short, such presumptions will understate racial and ethnic disadvantages found within the African immigrant population and provide a skewed picture of African immigrants' educational attainment.

Within labor markets the implications of racial and ethnic differences are equally important. Employers have known racial preferences that affect their hiring decisions, and the ways in which human capital is rewarded, that could be consequential for immigrants' labor market outcomes. Given this significance of race, Black and White Africans are likely to differentially encounter opportunities and constraints as they integrate into the US labor market. In these contexts, such differences may result in further disparities in their occupational attainment and employment outcomes. Arab racial identity may similarly be associated with additional patterns of inequality, such that non-Arab Africans may experience larger employment premiums compared to their Arab African counterparts. Persistent racial and ethnic differences will also have implications for earnings disparities. Previous studies have extensively described the earnings profiles of Black immigrants (Dodoo 1997). Nevertheless, they are largely limited by their failure to disaggregate the earnings of Africans in order to examine differences between Arabs and non-Arabs. Juxtaposing the earnings indicators for both groups, within race, may thus provide a more comprehensive perspective on the dynamics of economic assimilation among African immigrants.

At a more interpersonal level, race and ethnicity have implications for the formation of social relationships with US natives. Few indicators capture such relationships as well as those of intermarriage. These indicators are important because they reflect the erosion of cultural differences between the foreign and US-born populations. Yet, in the US social context, a number of factors can limit the erosion of these differences among immigrants with racial and ethnic minority characteristics. For example, there are prevailing notions of spousal desirability that consider potential White spouses more desirable than those who are Black (Fu 2001; Heaton and Jacobson 2000). Moreover, Arab social and cultural attributes are associated with Islamic stereotypes that can create barriers to the intermarriage prospects of Arab African immigrants. The high prevalence of racial endogamy in the marriage patterns of US racial groups also raises the question of whether intermarriage between Africans and US natives will also be racially circumscribed. Among African immigrants, therefore, racial and ethnic differences may affect the extent to which they are able to shift from traditional notions of marriage to more American perspectives as predicted by conventional notions of marital incorporation.

Finally, if racial and ethnic differences persist across multiple social and economic indicators, then a firm basis would be provided for the argument that Black and White Africans experience diverse pathways of incorporation into US society. The implications of these differences will be profound. Among other things, they will underscore the fact that there are important connections between the racial and ethnic inequalities observed among Africans in Africa and those found among African immigrants in the United States. Yet, persistent inequalities will also have implications that are policy related. For example, they will raise questions concerning what an economic disadvantage of Black Africans relative to White Africans implies for affirmative action policies. Furthermore, social inequalities will also have research implications. In particular, they will have ramifications for how research is conducted on African diaspora populations. Among other things, they will call for more nuanced understandings of how the African diaspora is defined. Such nuances will encourage the development of more comprehensive discourses on race and ethnic identity. In so doing, they will result in new perspective on how both factors influence the welfare of Africans living in western societies.

Theoretical Perspectives

S everal theoretical perspectives can be used to predict the expected socio-economic incorporation processes of Black and White African immigrants. Developing a more comprehensive framework for understanding these processes, however, requires a careful distinction between their pre- and post-migration determinants. For example, the antecedents of racial inequality in Africa are important for understanding the influence of Black-White premigration inequalities on the postimmigration social mobility of African immigrants. At the same time, conventional theories, which largely focus on post-immigration influences, discuss a range of contextual determinants that could either reinforce or exacerbate patterns of social stratification among Africans. These theories also provide important lenses through which inequalities among African immigrants can be understood. For example, variations in social class and human-capital endowments are known to independently affect immigrant incorporation outcomes (Portes and Borocz 1989; Waters and Jimenez 2005). Human-capital endowments refer to resources that are embedded in people (Becker 1962), specifically to skills, training, and individual-level attributes such as motivation, which help individuals be more productive. When human-capital variations occur among Africans, they can complicate the analysis of the extent to which race facilitates or impedes the social mobility of African immigrant subgroups.

Notwithstanding the multiplicity of determinants of incorporation, how-ever, research indicates that race, especially as pertains to Blackness, remains an important predictor of postimmigration incorporation differences (Bashi and McDaniel 1997; Alba and Nee 1997; Reitz and Sklar 1997; Zhou 1997). Moreover, the primacy of race as a determinant of successful incorporation has been recognized as a key feature of US social dynamics for more than a century. Early citizenship laws, for example, considered all "non-White" persons to be ineligible for US citizenship (Boswell 2003; Martinez 2006). Historically, perceptions of skin color differences have likewise had implications for determining which immigrant groups were more welcomed, since skin color differences were assumed to reflect differences in biological superiority. Gordon (1964) thus indicated that the rapid influx of southern European immigrants in the late 1800s generated significant discourses concerning the biological superiority of immigrants with lighter skin tones and fairer hair. In addition to skin tone differences, ethnic disparities have also had implications for the reception and incorporation of immigrant groups. In the early 1920s, for example, many US employers believed that Mexican immigrants were biologically suited for stoop labor (Sanchez 1997). Furthermore, towards the end of the nineteenth century, the immigration and settlement of Asian immigrant groups was discouraged by prevailing high levels of anti-Chinese and general anti-Asian sentiment (Kawanabe 1996; Lee 1989).

Before the 1960s, therefore, successful immigrant incorporation primarily depended on whether immigrants possessed a combination of White racial char-acteristics and a European ethnic ancestry. Boswell (2003) thus suggests that discrimination against non-White immigrants was so intense during this period that potential Black African migrants would have been difficult to persuade to settle in the United States, regardless of whether or not there were legal barriers to their immigration.

Race relations have improved since the mid-1960s, and there is now greater racial and ethnic diversity among contemporary immigrants. Despite these improvements, however, contemporary theorists underscore the unrelenting significance of race for creating differential patterns of immigrant success (Alba and Nee 1997; Bashi and McDaniel 1997; Zhou 1997). Furthermore, although discourses on immigrants' biological superiority, based on their physical characteristics, are largely on the decline, such variations, especially with regard to skin tone, are still fundamental for understanding their differential access to opportunity and resources.

Racially stratified patterns of immigrant incorporation therefore challenge traditional narratives of the incorporation process, which suggest that initial differences between immigrants and natives will disappear over the course of time. More recent theories expand on these concerns and their implications for the perpetuation of inequality across immigrant generations. Establishing conceptual relationships between race, ethnicity, and African immigrant incorporation can thus provide an important basis for interrogating these traditional narratives. Moreover, highlighting theoretical linkages between premigration racial stratification patterns in Africa and racial inequalities among African immigrants reinforces the significance of cross-continental linkages between Black-White inequalities in the United States and similar race-based inequalities in African countries.

PREMIGRATION RACIAL INEQUALITIES IN AFRICA

Historical evidence suggests that the origins of inequalities between Black and White African immigrants can be traced to the dynamics of racial stratification in their countries of origin. Although multiracial societies in Africa emerged over the course of several centuries, the significance of race for creating patterns of social stratification became apparent almost immediately after the start of large-scale European settlement on the continent. In general, initial contact between both groups was rapidly followed by the sociopolitical domination of Africans by White Europeans. By approximately the end of the second decade of the twentieth century, European governments had firmly consolidated their interests on the continent, and almost all African countries had been colonized.

Racial stratification resulting from European contact with Africans can be understood from a number of theoretical perspectives (e.g., Lieberson 1961; Noel 1968; Turner 1986). Lieberson's (1961) social stratification theory, for example, provided one of the first theoretical frameworks used for understanding the dynamics of racial inequality between White European settlers and Black African natives. His theory builds on the assumption that migrant groups, for example, White European settlers, have different racial characteristics than indigenous populations. Accordingly, if both groups come together in a contact situation characterized by differentials in their ability to impose change, race relations will result from the dual processes of *superordination* and *subordination*. In southern Africa, for example, Lieberson argues that White European superordination was driven, among other things, by their superior military technology. Correspondingly, the inability of Black Africans to resist the military power of European settlers resulted in the subordination of the former relative to the latter. Subsequent patterns of White domination of Blacks, according to Lieberson, are thus a product of group differences in the ability to influence the circumstances of the initial contact.

Noel (1968) offers a similar theoretical perspective for understanding racial and ethnic stratification processes. Like Lieberson, Noel incorporates the circumstances of the initial contact between groups. From Noel's perspective, however, power differentials during the initial contact represent just one of three determinants of subsequent stratification patterns. The other two are ethnocentrism and competition for resources. Noel, therefore, improves on Lieberson's framework by providing a context, (i.e., competition), within which groups' motivations for using power could be understood. Furthermore, he also highlights how perceptions concerning ethnic superiority mediate this process. Altogether, these attributes make Noel's thesis even more relevant for understanding the origins of racial stratification in premigration societies in Africa.

Consistent with Noel's theory, systematic European engagement of African societies was clearly driven by the search for resources and the acquisition of new territories (Ewans 2002; O'Toole 2007). This quest was institutionalized at the Berlin Conference of 1884, in which European powers partitioned Africa and developed a formal basis for creating colonial territories (Bassett 1994; Mutua 2000). Not surprisingly, the physical acquisition of land was done at the expense of Black African natives. For example, colonial laws were enacted to specifically decrease the ability of African peasants to compete with European producers (Berman 1984). Also consistent with Noel's theory was the tendency for the appropriation of lands to be facilitated by power differentials between White Europeans, with their sophisticated military technology, and Africans. Chege (1997), for example, notes that the success of the European colonial enterprise was guaranteed by their superior firepower. Finally, as predicted by Noel's third criteria for racial stratification, relationships between European settlers and Africans were also influenced by European ethnocentrism and their aversion towards "uncivilized" Africans (D. M. Hughes 2006). In colonial Zimbabwe, for example, the political ideology of the White-dominated Rhodesian Front was largely guided by its belief in the racial inferiority of Blacks relative to Whites (Musvoto 2009).

For much of the colonial period, therefore, racial differences were distinctively associated with the ownership of resources, differences in social status, and access to power. High-level positions in government and industry were thus systematically reserved for White Europeans (Chege 1997). In Kenya, Zimbabwe, and Tanzania, White Europeans also had access to the most fertile and productive agricultural lands (Chege 1997; Hammer 2010). Significantly, Power

(1993) suggests that racial stratification in Africa was sometimes expressed as an explicit policy of European colonial powers. In particular, he notes that one of the expressed objectives of the British colonial consul in central Africa was to see the region governed by Whites, developed by Indians (i.e., Asian Indians), and worked by Blacks.

As could be expected, racial inequalities during the colonial period formed the basis for subsequent patterns of inequality now observed between contemporary White and Black Africans. In Zimbabwe and Kenya, for example, Black Africans still face economic disadvantages compared to their White African counterparts (D. M. Hughes 2006; Gordon 1981; Laakso 2002). South African Blacks also continue to have lower incomes and are more likely to live in poverty than South African Whites (Klasen 1997). In terms of residential patterns, research indicates that contemporary White Kenyans are disproportionately represented in the wealthy suburban neighborhoods of Nairobi (Hoffmann 2010). Nyamweru (2001) also suggests that despite the decline in White influence in Kenya, White Kenyans still exert a significant level of political influence in the country.

White African economic influence has particularly been resilient in terms of their control of the means of production. By the end of the twentieth century, for example, three White-owned companies in South Africa accounted for about 76 percent of the capitalized stock on the Johannesburg stock exchange (Chege 1997). White Zambian economic interests further control a significant proportion of the hotel infrastructure supporting the country's safari industry (Dreike 2007). In countries such as Zimbabwe and South Africa, however, some of the economic prowess of White Africans has been eroded by the recent policies of the Black political class, or by transitions to Black majority rule.

At the country level, the European colonial enterprise has additional implications for understanding premigration racial inequalities in African societies. In particular, because the colonization process enterprise was driven by the search for natural resources, White settlement is now largely concentrated in Africa's more developed countries. Some of the most favorable country-level socioeconomic indicators in Africa are now found in the major origin countries of White African immigrants. For example, World Bank estimates show higher standards of living, incomes, and education in South Africa, Mozambique, and Namibia than in majority Black African countries such as Nigeria and Ghana (World Bank 2010). Overall, these patterns suggest that compared to White African immigrants, Black Africans are more likely to originate from Africa's poor and least developed countries.

Race and Stratification in Arab African Origin Countries

The origins of racial stratification in Africa's Arab societies are slightly different from those found elsewhere in Africa. For example, although multiracial societies in southern Africa are a product of White European migration and settlement, those in North Africa trace their origins to two main historical sources: White Arab migration and settlement from the Arabian Peninsula and the forced migration of Black Africans during the trans-Saharan slave trade. Lieberson's (1961) stratification theory is, however, still useful for understanding Arab African stratification patterns and the subsequent dynamics of racial inequality in those societies. For example, the lower status of Black Arabs compared to their White Arab counterparts could be associated with the process of *indigenous* superordination. This process is distinct from the process of *migrant* superordination that explains White European domination of Blacks in southern Africa. As Lieberson argues, indigenous superordination typically occurs in societies with a long history of slavery that also have powerful native populations that exert their dominance on less powerful migrant, slave populations. A major consequence of indigenous superordination is that the descendants of slaves remain subordinate and continue to have comparatively low levels of social status even after the end of institutionalized slavery.

Several perspectives on the consequences of slavery for stratification processes in Africa's Arab societies are, however, found in the literature. For example, Mazuri (1973) posits that there were more tolerant racial attitudes governing relationships between Arab slave-traders and their Black slaves compared to the respective attitudes of slave owners towards slaves in North America. Another difference between the two contexts, according to Mazuri, lies in their degree of acceptance of interracial marriages. Such marriages were prohibited in the United States but were generally more accepted in historical Arab African societies. Some Arab settlers and slave owners, for example, married Black African wives and had children by them. Mazuri notes, however, that despite the absence of nuptial restrictions on the basis of race, family prestige among Arab Africans was determined, among other things, on the basis of lighter shades of skin color. According to Deng (2006), however, religious identity was more important than race as a basis for social stratification in multiracial Arab African societies. In these contexts, Deng indicates, the acceptance of Islam and being culturally Arabized elevated the social status of Black Muslims, while their non-Muslim counterparts remained legitimate targets for enslavement. Other scholars, however, suggest that the role of Islam in Arab social stratification is misunderstood since the purchasing and transportation of Black slaves by White Arab slave-traders was largely done in violation of Islamic principles (El Hamel 2010; Mrad-Dali 2010).

Surprisingly, contemporary patterns of racial stratification in Arab African countries are not well documented in the literature, due to limited research on stratification and inequality in Arab countries. Some available studies, however, provide evidence of a continued disadvantage of Black Arabs relative to White Arabs in predominantly Arab African countries. According to El Hamel (2010), for example, Black Arabs in Morocco experience systematic patterns of discrimination as a result of their racial minority status (El Hamel 2008). Furthermore, Mrad-Dali (2005) asserts that Black Arabs in Tunisia now constitute the majority of the country's underprivileged social class (2005). Washington (1990) similarly observes that Black Egyptians face significant social disadvantages stemming from existing skin color prejudices in Egypt. In general, these patterns suggest that compared to their White Arab-African counterparts, Black Arab immigrants from Africa experienced a greater level of social disadvantage in their origin countries before migrating to the United States.

Race and the Incorporation of Immigrants into US Society

Theoretical descriptions of postimmigration incorporation processes typically focus on the question of whether social and cultural differences between immigrants and natives disappear as immigrants become more incorporated. These inquiries have their origins in sociological descriptions of the assimilation processes of European immigrants who arrived in the United States between 1880 and 1920. For much of the previous century, therefore, theories of immigrant incorporation were grounded in the experiences of European immigrants. As a result, the trajectory of European immigrants who arrived during this period provided the primary benchmark used in research on the incorporation patterns of subsequent immigrants groups (Waters and Jaminez 2005).

Gordon's (1964) classical assimilation theory encapsulates this approach by suggesting that immigrants are incorporated into the United States in a dynamic process spanning three generations. Second-generation immigrants, that is, the children of first-generation immigrants, are thus more assimilated than their parents, and by the third generation, the descendants of immigrants are expected to be fully assimilated into American life. This perspective suggests that greater exposure to US society increases immigrant assimilation. As such, it has also been interpreted as implying that first-generation immigrants (i.e., the foreign born) can also become more assimilated with increasing exposure to the United States, measured by their years of residence (Ford 1990; Schultz 1998). As immigrants become incorporated, they are expected to move from acculturation processes to complete structural assimilation. The former describes the process by which immigrants adopt the language and cultural values of the United States, while the later is characterized by the entry of immigrants into American organizations and institutions. Structural assimilation, according to Gordon, is thus the *"keystone of the arch of assimilation"* (Gordon 1964, 81) since it is accompanied by the disappearance of the ethnic group and its distinctive values.

The classical assimilation framework has, however, been criticized for, among other things, using White Anglo-Saxon Protestants as the cultural standard that determines the direction of immigrant assimilation processes (e.g., Alba and Nee 1997). Thus, if it is used to examine the outcomes of African immigrants, successful incorporation among both Black and White Africans will be assessed by the extent to which both groups conform to the cultural standards of US-born Whites. Since the mid-1960s, however, studies have consistently shown that contemporary immigrant groups have more diverse patterns of incorporation.

Segmented assimilation theory describes an approach that reflects these variations, arguing against a single pathway of incorporation among immigrants to the United States (Portes and Zhou 1993; Zhou 1997). Indeed, segmented assimilation processes include pathways that allow for the fact that some immigrants, like early European immigrants, will be incorporated into increasingly higher social status and have their cultural differences with US natives disappear. More importantly, however, it emphasizes the fact that some immigrant groups will not be incorporated into similar patterns of upward mobility. In contrast, these groups will experience a reproduction of their disadvantage relative to US natives as they become integrated. With increasing exposure to the United States, less favorable trajectories will be observed in their socioeconomic indicators, such as levels of poverty, schooling, and residential patterns (Hirschman 2001; Iceland 2009). These disparate incorporation pathways found across immigrant groups largely reflect the fact that US society offers different possibilities to immigrants based on a number of factors. Among these are factors such as immigrants' social class, their contexts of reception, and their race (Portes and Zhou 1993; Zhou 1997).

In their theory of race and immigration, Bashi and McDaniel (1997) further expand on the implications of race for Black immigrants' social mobility. They argue that Black immigrants, upon arrival, are forced into a racial stratification system based on a fixed American perception of race. A critical feature of this system is that it disregards ethnic differences between Black immigrants and US-born Blacks, classifying both groups as Black based on an overarching social construction of race. Bashi and McDaniel therefore argue that Black immigrants, like US-born Blacks, occupy the bottom of the US racial hierarchy. As a result, both groups are expected to face similar prejudices based on their racial minority status irrespective of their differences in immigration status. A major implication of this proposition is that the significance of race for understanding the social mobility of Black African immigrants cannot be identified by comparing their outcomes with those of US-born Blacks. Instead, as Bashi and McDaniel assert, these implications are better understood by comparing Black immigrants, located at the bottom of the racial hierarchy, with a racial reference group, such as White immigrants, found at the top of the hierarchy.

Incorporation differences between Black and White Africans can thus be informed by the tenets of both Bashi and McDaniel's approach and segmented assimilation theory. Both theories capture the intractable nature of boundaries based on racial phenotypes, especially those separating Blacks and Whites, and point to the influence of race in circumscribing the possibilities available to immigrants. Surprisingly, however, comparisons of the outcomes of White and Black immigrants from similar regional origins are generally limited. Where available, such comparisons largely focus on racial differences among Hispanic immigrant populations. Prior research among Mexican immigrants, for example, identifies schooling disadvantages among immigrants with darker skin tones compared to those with lighter skin tones (Murguia and Telles 1996). Black Cuban immigrants have also been found to have less favorable patterns of economic assimilation than White Cuban immigrants (Zavodny 2003). Skin tone differences have also been reported to have similar implications for wage differentials among Hispanic groups, broadly defined (Frank and Akresh 2010). On the whole, these findings are important for understanding the socioeconomic implications of skin color differences among African immigrants. As noted by Alba and Nee (1997), darker skin tones, in combination with any apparent connection with US-born Blacks, create a racist barrier for Black Africans that is not encountered by immigrants of other racial groups.

Arab Immigrants and US Racial Classification Systems

The relevance of theories of incorporation highlighting the significance of race for understanding the outcomes of Arab immigrants has not been systematically examined in previous studies. This partly reflects the fact that racial and ethnic labels used in the classification of Arab immigrants have varied considerably over the past century. Official classifications of Arabs in the United States have also been driven by the fact that Arab immigration streams have historically been dominated by White or lighter-skinned Arabs. Yet even more important is the fact that Arab Americans have a long history of embracing a White racial identity. Kayyali (2006), for example, argues that as far back as 1908, Arab Americans enjoyed many of the privileges associated with Whiteness. However, legal disputes concerning whether Arab Americans could be defined as Whites sometimes resulted in contradictory rulings (Gualtieri 2001; Naber 2000). In 1914, for example, US courts acknowledged that Syrian Arab immigrants were Caucasian, but denied them the benefits of citizenship, which, according to the courts, was intended for people of European descent (Naber 2000). Although this ruling was subsequently reversed in the 1923, Arab claims to Whiteness were generally revealed in the arguments used in the legal processes. Syrian Arab groups, for example, argued that as Semites, they were Caucasian and therefore should be consider as White Americans (Kayyali 2006).

Arab American claims to Whiteness and their institutional classification as Whites are also found in recent studies on the incorporation of Arab immigrant groups. However, both processes are found in the literature on predominantly White Arab immigrant groups. Arab immigrants with Caucasian features thus increasingly self-identify as "White" in what some scholars consider to be a strategic attempt to avoid the stigma associated with racial minority status (Wingfield 2006). Ajrouch and Jamal (2007), however, observe what they consider to be segmented patterns of Arab self-identification. Their study reported that while some Arabs identify themselves as Whites, others simply preferred to use a general Arab American identity. Somewhat contrary evidence is further suggested by scholars who maintain that White Arab immigrants feel a stronger attachment to their origin countries than to US racial markers (McDermott and Samson 2005). Similarly, other scholars argue that some White Arabs resist the classification of Whiteness (Ajrouch and Jamal 2007; Naber 2000). Resistance to the White racial marker is, however, unlikely to affect the skin color advantage of White Arabs relative to Black Arab immigrants in their interactions with US natives. Research on Black Arab immigrants points to similar patterns of resistance to their being classified by a hegemonic Black racial identity (Fabos 2008). These attempts have likewise been unsuccessful in shielding Black Arab immigrants from racial prejudices, given the influence of Western social constructions of race that relegate people with darker skin tones to the bottom strata of society.

Another perspective on the racial classification of Arab immigrants is found in scholarly debates concerning whether Arabs should be considered a separate racial group or as simply an ethnic group. Gold (2004) argues that Arab Americans are a distinct racial group whose incorporation processes cannot be understood on the basis of the predominant Black-White model of racial inequality. Given the significance of group differences in skin color for informing constructions of race, however, classifying Arab immigrants as a unified racial group is generally problematic. Arab immigrants, like Hispanics, are more unified by cultural characteristics than by similarities in racial phenotype. Increasingly, therefore, studies on the incorporation of Arab immigrants tend to classify them using an ethnic rather than a racial label (Read 2003; Shamhan 2001). Arab racial variations documented in the literature (Al-Khatib 2006; Assali, Khamaysi, and Birnbaum 1997; Ezza and Libis 2010; Fabos 2008; Sirtima 2009; Middleton and O'Keefe 2006) also conceptually undermine the notion of a distinct Arab incorporation pattern that is insensitive to differences in race. Consequently, racial differences among Arabs must be interrogated in studies on their social incorporation processes.

THE LATIN AMERICANIZATION OF RACE

Bonilla-Silva (2002; 2004) also challenges the relevance of the Black-White racial framework and incorporates Arabs in his more extensive Latin Americanization model of racial stratification. His main argument is that rather than having a Black-White racial dichotomy, the US racial stratification system is based on a three-tier classification system. At the top of the system are Whites, followed by honorary Whites, and the collective Black. The Latin Americanization model is also distinct from other frameworks because it uses a collective Arab American racial identity and classifies all Arab Americans as part of the honorary White category. In doing so, Bonilla-Silva inadvertently fails to incorporate Arab racial differences into his schema. Other members of the honorary White category include Asians and other immigrant groups that have phenotypic similarities with non-Hispanic Whites. Significantly, Bonilla-Silva asserts that the negative racial impact of anti-Arab discrimination following the September 11, 2001, terrorist attacks does not imply that they are found at the very bottom of the US racial hierarchy. Despite these injustices, he argues, Arab Americans (i.e., White Arab Americans) do not identify themselves with other racial minorities and thus face a distinct set of circumstances compared to, for example, Blacks.

The Latin Americanization model has been criticized for a number of reasons. Sue (2009) challenges its basic tenets by arguing that Latin American racial categories, which the model tries to replicate, are based on skin color gradations rather than discrete racial groups. The model has also been criticized for understating the continued significance of the Black/non-Black divide. Marrow (2009), for example, observes that while darker-skinned Hispanic immigrants see the social barriers between themselves and Whites as permeable, they systematically adopt strategies that reinforce their social distance relative to Blacks. Herring (2002) also criticizes the model by arguing that although empirical tests confirm some of its key hypotheses, they also show that Blacks are not always at the bottom of the US racial hierarchy. The model has also been criticized for failing to incorporate the fluidity of race. Accordingly, Rockquemore and Arend (2002) assert that individuals in intermediate racial categories who look White have the liberty of choosing how they identify themselves within the US racial classification system.

In spite of these criticisms, the model's three-tier system makes important contributions to the study of racial hierarchies. Among these is the fact that it allows individuals from similar ethnic groups to fall into different categories in the three-tier system, based on intraethnic differences in skin color. Accordingly, although White Hispanics find themselves in the top racial stratum, "White," Black Hispanics such as Black Puerto-Ricans are classified in the model's bottom strata as part of the collective Black (Forman, Goar, and Lewis 2002). This categorization schema can therefore be used to classify Arab African immigrants into different levels in the stratification hierarchy based on differences in their racial characteristics.

Race, Ethnicity, and Formation Processes

Another perspective on race relevant for understanding inequalities among African immigrants focuses on the dynamics of sociohistorical processes. This perspective emphasizes the fact that what constitutes race has been differentially defined in previous decades, and in the process shifted to accommodate prevailing social and political exigencies. Omi and Winant (1994) explicate this perspective in their theory of racial formation processes. These formation processes describe the sociohistorical dynamics in which racial categories are created, transformed, or destroyed. They note that the ethnicity paradigm is at the core of the modern sociology of race. However, what's considered to be an ethnic group has itself changed across time. Before the 1930s, for example, the concept was mainly used to contest biological conceptions of race and their presupposition that racial inferiority is based on a natural order in which Whites are superior to non-Whites. After the 1930s race primarily emerged as a social category and was considered to be one of the many characteristics of ethnic groups. Scholars of critical race theory have partly extended this discourse by emphasizing the "social construction" thesis, which notes the disconnection between race and biological attributes as well as the fact that race, as a social construction, can be subject to manipulation (Delgado and Stefancic 2001). The emergence of race as a social construct also corresponded with the expansion of studies on assimilation processes. By the post-1965 period, racial formation discourses had further developed to include an increasing focus on issues related to group rights (Omi and Winant 1994).

Naber (2008) incorporates this racial formation perspective to conceptualize recent trends in the racialization of Arab Americans. Her main argument is that shifts in the conceptualization of race the Second World War period have coincided with a period of growing anti-Arab discourses. For example, as US military and economic involvement in the Middle East increased in the 1960s, Arabs became increasingly racialized as the "other." During the oil wars in the 1970s they were considered to be "greedy Arab oil sheiks." In the 1980s and 1990s, however, Arabs became much more racialized as terrorists. Naber also maintains that because racialization processes become more intense during periods of crisis, such as among Japanese Americans during the Second World War, more recent shifts in the racialization of Arabs became more intense following September 11, 2001.

Racial formation perspectives generally have a number of implications for understanding issues of inequality among Black and White African immigrants. As Omi and Winant (1994) suggest, the ethnicity paradigm that emerged in the second phase of the racial formation process and its emphasis on conventional assimilation dynamics is limited. Immigrants who are racial minorities, such as Black non-Arab and Arab Africans, will still remain distinct from the White majority regardless of whether or not they fully adopt White values and norms. Naber's formation perspective on the evolution of Arab ethnicity further underscores the possibility that Arab African immigrants will encounter significantly more constraints than non-Arab Africans during their incorporation processes in the post–September 11 context. Yet she also maintains that beyond the disadvantages associated with anti-Arab racism, consideration must also be given to the ways in which "race" itself provides access to opportunities and possibilities to groups that have traditionally been considered to be non-White. As she points out, not all Arab Americans can pass as White. For those who can (e.g., White Arab Africans), their ability to identify with Whiteness can produce significant opportunities for social advancement. Nevertheless, similar opportunities will not available to other Arab immigrants such as Black Arab Africans who identify themselves differently.

BLACK EXCEPTIONALISM AND THE RETURN OF THE COLOR LINE

Notwithstanding the multiplicity of theories of racial stratification, scholars are increasingly returning to Du Bois's (1903) position on the significance of color lines for understanding contemporary patterns of inequality. One such group of scholars focuses on Blackness as a unique form of racial disadvantage distinctively different from other forms of racial minority status (Lee and Bean 2007; Sears et al. 2003). This perspective suggests that regardless of nativity status, Blacks collectively encounter higher levels of prejudice, disadvantage, and inequality compared to all non-Black groups. As Yancey (2003) argues, the experience of Blacks is qualitatively distinct. As a result, although lighter-skinned immigrants such as the Irish and Asians, like Blacks, have a history of being considered racially inferior to non-Hispanic Whites, they have successfully circumvented these disadvantages by subsequently assimilating into Whiteness. The Black racial identity, in contrast, is less fluid and is associated with social disadvantages that continue to persist across time.

Black exceptionalism is generally supported by evidence showing that social and economic outcomes are increasingly differentiated along a Black/non-Black divide. For example, Kroeger and Williams (2011) indicate that in interracial unions, relationships with Blacks attract higher levels of stigma and disapproval than do relationships with non-Blacks. Similarly, Lee and Bean (2010) found that racial status is not a significant issue in interracial marriages between Whites and Asians. On the contrary, they observe that non-Black families are more likely to oppose interracial marriage with Blacks as a result of its association with perceptions of downward mobility. Parisi, Lichter, and Taquino (2011) also support the Black exceptionalism framework with findings showing extreme levels of residential segregation of Blacks relative to non-Blacks. They argue that their findings suggest that non-Black groups such as Whites and Asians are now increasingly trying to distance themselves from Blacks.

Recent immigration studies also report stratification patterns consistent with a Black/non-Black divide. Hall (2010), for example, finds exceptionally high levels of residential segregation among Black African and Caribbean immigrants consistent with the notion of Black exceptionalism. Sears and Savalie (2006) also observe that Black immigrants have distinct political assimilation trajectories compared to non-Black immigrants. In terms of income, Daneshvary and Schwer (1994) report that non-Black immigrants collectively earn 22 percent more than Black immigrants. In addition, Lee and Bean (2010) argue that immigration from Latin America and Asia contributes to the reinforcement of the Black/non-Black racial divide. In their perspective, this stems from the fact that these new immigrants try to maintain their distinctiveness from Blacks in ways that mirror the large social distance between Blacks and Whites.

SUMMARY AND IMPLICATIONS

A central argument made in this analysis is that theoretical perspectives derived from the experiences of non-African immigrants have limited relevance for studying the outcomes of African immigrants. In contrast to conventional frameworks, recent theories incorporating the significance of race are more appropriate for understanding the differential incorporation experiences of Black and White African immigrants. In order to fully understand racial differences in the social incorporation pathways of African immigrants, the significance of premigration racial inequalities in African societies must also be well understood. Similarly, stratification theories highlighting the significance of both race and ethnic differences are particularly important for predicting expected patterns of social inequality among African immigrant groups.

Given racial and ethnic differences among African immigrant groups, theories of incorporation and racial stratification would suggest that African immigrant race-ethnic groups are unlikely to have similar patterns of incorporation into society. Instead, these theories predict differential socioeconomic trajectories among African immigrants during the incorporation process. In general, these disparate pathways will reflect a combination of the influence of premigration racial inequalities and the renewed significance of race after arrival in the US social context. Better premigration access to human capital among White than Black Africans, for example, implies that White Africans are more likely than

Black Africans to arrive with the kinds of resources known to facilitate social mobility. Instructively, however, if such socioeconomic differences are the principal determinants of the White African advantage relative to Black Africans, racial inequalities should disappear after human-capital differentials are accounted for. Incorporation and racial stratification theories suggest, however, that White Africans will continue to have a postimmigration advantage over Black Africans because the US postimmigration context is one in which race is associated with differential access to opportunity.

Since Black and White Africans are further differentiated by Arab ethnicity, the outcomes of African immigrants are not expected to strictly conform to the triracial hierarchy predicted by the Latin Americanization model. Nevertheless, the model can be modified to define the racial and ethnic stratification patterns expected to be observed among African immigrants. Non-Arab White African immigrants, for example, are expected be found at the top of the hierarchy since they experience the advantages associated with Whiteness and are able to avoid the disadvantages stemming from negative US perceptions of Arab ethnicity. These perceptions and their association with anti-Arab prejudices are, however, expected to lead to less favorable patterns of incorporation among White Arabs than among non-Arab Whites. Furthermore, because the racial characteristics of White Arabs are similar to those of US non-Hispanic Whites, White Arabs are expected to have more positive socioeconomic outcomes than both Black African immigrant groups. Among Black Africans, however, more favorable outcomes are expected to be observed among Blacks with non-Arab than Arab ethnic origins. These predicted patterns are consistent with the expectation that within both the Arab and non-Arab African immigrant populations, there will be a clear color line underlying a Black African racial disadvantage. The extent to which these stratification patterns are supported by empirical evidence is systematically examined in subsequent chapters. Confirmation of their existence will provide a useful basis for understanding the dynamics of social mobility among African immigrants during their incorporation into the US social mainstream.

Educational Attainment and Postimmigration Schooling Progress

T he educational profile of immigrants provides important insights into their human-capital endowments and their expected trajectory of socio-economic incorporation. As critical human-capital indicators, schooling levels can predict whether or not immigrants will experience upward mobility trends as they become integrated into society. In practical terms, education is important for providing access to financially rewarding opportunities in the labor market. In most cases, therefore, immigrants with high levels of education are more successful than other immigrants in securing well-paid jobs and improving their economic welfare. Yet, the payoffs to schooling extend beyond more immediate economic considerations. High levels of schooling are positively associated with language assimilation, facilitate neighborhood integration, and influence the formation of interpersonal relationships between immigrants and the native-born (Carliner 2000; Qian and Lichter 2001; Hall 2009). Immigrant groups with low schooling levels can therefore face significant obstacles in their efforts to integrate into their communities.

Among immigrants and natives, however, opportunities for acquiring education and overall levels of educational attainment are considerably circumscribed by race and ethnicity. Yet despite increasing attention to the educational outcomes of African immigrants, systematic examinations of racial variations in their education attainment are limited. In general, the significance of education for understanding immigrant incorporation processes points to the need for new studies examining whether the educational pathways to social mobility available to Africans are differentiated by race. This process requires a closer look at inequalities in the educational profiles of Black and White African immigrants, whether such inequalities are further differentiated by Arab ethnicity, and the implications of these differences for overall socioeconomic incorporation processes.

By focusing on the significance of immigration status and race for understanding educational inequalities among African immigrants, the analysis brings needed clarity to discourses on their achievement patterns. These discourses center around two broad perspectives. The first focuses on the overall educational profile of African immigrants and highlights the fact that they typically have higher levels of educational attainment than the US-born (Kaba 2007). While this perspective is supported by empirical evidence, it is nevertheless limited by its failure to distinguish between the outcomes of Black and White Africans or interrogate the outcomes of Africans of Arab and non-Arab origin. Focusing on the larger African immigrant population rather than on racial subgroups also understates the significance of race for immigrants' educational experiences after immigration. In other words, racial schooling differences among Africans enrolled in US institutions can provide useful insights concerning whether or not racial minority status results in bifurcated patterns of African educational incorporation into US society.

A second perspective on African immigrant educational outcomes draws from decades-old research on historical and structural constraints on achievement among US-born Blacks. In particular, comparisons between US-born Blacks and Black immigrants are now used in debates concerning the continued significance of racial minority status as a constraint on achievement. Some interpretations of the comparatively higher levels of schooling of Black Africans relative to US-born Blacks suggest that the Black immigrant experience implies that race is no longer a barrier to schooling. Instead, alternative frameworks used to explain the educational disadvantage of US-born Blacks understate the significance of race as a barrier to achievement by focusing on countercultural influences as major determinants of their lower levels of schooling. Conclusions about race based on comparisons between immigrant and US-born Blacks can, however, be misleading. As argued later in the chapter, such comparisons are limited by their inability to capture specific racial barriers encountered by Black, but not White, Africans during the educational incorporation process.

In general, therefore, the analysis presented in this chapter attempts to achieve several objectives. First, it documents existing knowledge on educational achievement among African immigrants in order to provide a critical overview of the dynamics and determinants of their educational attainment levels. Second, the question of the Black African schooling advantage in comparison to US Blacks is systematically examined, with particular attention given to the limits of conventional frameworks used to explain this disparity. Third, given the limited focus on the race and ethnic schooling inequalities among contemporary African immigrants, educational inequalities between Black and White Africans of Arab and non-Arab origins are empirically examined. Evidence on postimmigration schooling achievement of African youth is then used to suggest that Black Africans still experience a range of disadvantages associated with racial minority status that constrict their levels of achievement relative to those of White Africans. The implications of racial and ethnic educational inequalities for understanding the educational incorporation of African immigrants are then discussed.

RACE AND EDUCATIONAL ATTAINMENT IN THE AFRICAN-BORN POPULATION

Recent reviews of the human-capital characteristics of African immigrants consistently demonstrate that Africans are quite distinct from the US-born in terms of their educational attainment. Kaba (2007), for example, reviewing evidence from the 1990s, lauds the fact that African immigrants in general are among the most educated groups in the United States. The *Journal of Blacks in Higher Education* (JBHE) uses similar evidence to reach a more categorical conclusion. In their view, African immigrants are the nation's most highly educated group (JBHE 2000). In particular, its analysis indicates that African immigrants are more likely to graduate from high school or have college degrees than the US-born and immigrants from Asia and Europe. More recent evidence further confirms the persistence of the African schooling advantage among selected immigrant groups. For example, immigrants from Kenya, Tanzania, and Uganda have been found to be more likely than the US-born to have college-level credentials (Mbaya, Mrina, and Levin 2007). Other recent studies similarly confirm the exceptional average schooling levels of African immigrants (e.g., Kent 2007; Wilson and Habecker 2008). Not surprisingly, these observations have again been used in recent years to suggest that African immigrants are the smartest Americans (Page 2007).

From a human-capital perspective, it seems clear that at least in terms of schooling, African immigrants have attributes predictive of favorable patterns of postimmigration mobility. After all, favorable schooling outcomes among other immigrant groups, such as those from Asia, have been foundational to their successful socioeconomic incorporation into the United States (Xie and Goyette 2003). Racial variations among Africans, however, raise significant questions regarding the reliability of the human-capital model for predicting their subsequent patterns of postimmigration success. For example, average schooling levels among African immigrants provide an incomplete picture of their expected social and economic trajectory; they fail to consider race-based educational inequalities they experience both in their origin societies and after arriving in the United States.

Another limitation of previous studies is the fact that they seemingly conflate the outcomes of African immigrants with those of Black African immigrants and the educational heterogeneity found among Africans. Indeed, the *Journal of Blacks in Higher Education* tempered its report on the exceptional schooling of Africans with a caveat indicating that it "did not know how many of the African immigrants are White . . . [and] . . . how many of the African immigrants are non-blacks. . . . from other Arab nations of North Africa" (JBHE 2000, 61). Instructively, limited available studies of African immigrant subgroups suggest that there is considerable educational variation among Africans. For example, studies on the educational outcomes of Arab Africans show that immigrants from Egypt also have schooling levels that exceed US averages (Brittingham and De la Cruz 2005). On the other hand, specific African refugee immigrant groups, such as those from Sudan, tend to have lower levels of schooling than the US-born population (Power and Shandy 1998). In general, investigations of racial schooling differences among Black and White Arab African immigrants are unavailable. Similarly, there are limited systematic comparisons of the educational profiles of Black and White Africans. When available, however, race-based comparisons point to the existence of racial schooling inequalities among the African immigrant population. For example, some studies indicate that Black Africans are slightly less likely to have college degrees than White Africans (Dodoo and Takyi 2002; Kohlellon and Eule 2003), while more recent evidence suggests that the Black African disadvantage is becoming more distinct (Thomas, 2012). In the absence of systematic comparisons of educational achievement among Black and White Africans, previous studies inadvertently discount the disadvantage of Black Africans and understate the degree of educational inequality found among African immigrants.

Also missing from studies on the educational achievement of African immigrants is the fact that a significant number of Black Africans originate from multiracial origin societies with considerable colonial legacies of schooling inequality. In Zimbabwe, for example, schools with more economic resources are still located in predominantly White neighborhoods (Mpofu, Thomas, and Chan 2008). Furthermore, Black Zimbabwean students taught by White teachers have lower levels of academic self-esteem than their White Zimbabwean peers (Mpofu and Watkins 1997). Similar schooling inequalities are found in South Africa, where, as part of the apartheid system, White schools received higher levels of financial support than Black South African schools. This legacy of Black disadvantage extends into the postapartheid period, now characterized by significantly high levels of racial schooling inequalities in contemporary South Africa (Fiske and Ladd 2004). However, Zimbabwe and South Africa are not alone in terms of their White African schooling advantage relative to Black Africans. In post-independent Namibia, White students still attend schools with more resources than those attended by their Black Namibian counterparts (Herdin and Nilsson 2009). Focusing on overall African immigrant schooling levels therefore discounts a different kind of inequality generally originating from contexts in which Whites had privileged access to better-quality schooling.

BLACK AFRICAN EDUCATIONAL ACHIEVEMENT COMPARED TO OTHER BLACKS

Notwithstanding the limitations of previous studies, it is still true that levels of educational attainment among Black African immigrants are quite high. For example, Black Africans have higher levels of schooling than Black immigrants from the Caribbean and South America (Capps, McCabe, and Fix 2011). As mentioned earlier, Black Africans also have higher levels of educational attainment than US-born Blacks (Kent 2007). The proportion of Black Africans with undergraduate, graduate, and professional degrees also exceeds those for all immigrants, the US-born, and the Black immigrant averages (Capps, McCabe, and Fix 2011). Indeed, the high level of educational achievement among Black African immigrants is the principal factor driving the overall Black immigrant schooling advantage relative to US-born Blacks (Logan and Deane 2003).

Reactions to the high levels of schooling among Black Africans have generally been positive. Yet these positive reactions are based on questionable assumptions concerning the implications of Black immigrants' educational attainment. Freeman (2002) and Page (2007), for example, consider Black immigrants a type of new model minority group. However, as demonstrated later in the analysis, the evidence shows a consistent racial disadvantage among Black

Africans that provides critical evidence needed to reject the Black immigrant model minority hypothesis. Other commentaries are even more celebratory and disturbingly suggest that given their extraordinary achievements, Black Africans can serve as exemplars to US-born Blacks as models of ethnic minority success (Pierre 2004). Some of these reactions appear to be driven by the need for new evidence contradicting commonly held stereotypes about the intellectual inferiority of Blacks. Thus, Hayes (2009) considers data on Africans as providing such evidence: "Those of you who secretly believe that Black folk can't learn too good . . . take a look at the data on true Africans who've immigrated to the US." Claims associated with the model minority status of Black Africans are, however, problematic, and their specific limitations are reviewed later in the chapter. Before that discussion, it is necessary to examine why African immigrants generally have high levels of education. These explanations provide a basis for distinguishing between the pre- and postimmigration educational outcomes of African immigrants and their implications for the association between race and schooling during the incorporation process.

WHY ARE AFRICAN IMMIGRANT EDUCATIONAL LEVELS SO HIGH?

The first explanation for the high levels of schooling of African immigrants is associated with declining economic trends in Africa in the last two decades of the previous century. As a result of consequent decreases in income and rising unemployment, African graduates, attracted by economic opportunities elsewhere, migrated in large numbers to other countries in a process now referred to as the "brain drain." The concept of the brain drain is used to describe the large-scale departure of highly educated individuals from their countries of origin, typically in search of greener pastures. Similar processes have been documented in other developing regions; however, African countries are believed to have the highest rates of brain drain in the world (Docquier, Lohest, and Marfouk 2007). Many of these highly educated Africans come from origin countries with significant White populations (e.g., South Africa), from Black Africa, and Arab African countries. In general, the migration of highly educated Africans now accounts for a substantial proportion of international migration from Africa to the United States, Canada, and countries in Europe.

Changes in US immigration policy have also had a significant bearing on the educational characteristics of recent African immigrants to the United States. In particular, the introduction of the US Diversity Visa (DV) program as part of the Immigration Act of 1990 provided a new official channel of immigration for highly educated Africans, resulting in the large-scale departure of some of Africa's brightest minds (Lobo 2001; 2006). In fact, African immigration through the DV program is now a significant contributor to overall increases in African immigration to the United States (Thomas 2011a). Although the program was originally geared towards increasing the immigration of individuals from nontraditional sending countries, Africans have disproportionately benefited from the increased admissions resulting from the program since its inception (Newton 2005). Another consequence of the 1990 Immigration Act is that it increased the number of employment visas available to potential immigrants. Along with similarly educated immigrants from other countries, highly educated Africans have thus been increasingly admitted to the United States under employment preferences in recent years. Since 1990, for example, the number of Africans immigrating to the United States through employment preferences has increased by at least 100 percent (Lobo 2006).

A more contested view on the high achievement of African immigrants focuses on schooling disparities between Black Africans and US-born Blacks, and suggests that cultural differences between the groups explain these disparities. One variant of this perspective is that Black Africans, as voluntary minorities, are less constrained by the schooling disadvantages found among involuntary minority groups such as US-born Blacks (Ogbu 1987). As a result of their longer history of subjugation by the dominant White population, involuntary minorities are assumed to have behavioral practices of cultural inversion and oppositional norms that negatively affect schooling. Over the years, however, the validity of cultural explanations has been contested in empirical studies (Ainsworth-Darnell and Downey 1998). Yet culture-based explanations are found in recent suggestions that Black immigrants have unique attributes, which help them succeed, that US-born Blacks generally lack (Rimer and Arenson 2004). Since cultural explanations tend to focus on postimmigration schooling experiences, they are also limited in their ability to address why Black Africans arrive in the United States with high levels of schooling. Continued inferences about the unique attributes of Black Africans, however, reinforce the myth of the Black African model minority; that is, Black African immigrants have been able to overcome the racial barriers that have historically constrained educational achievement among US-born Blacks.

ARE BLACK AFRICAN IMMIGRANTS MODEL MINORITIES?

Considering Black African immigrants as a new model minority group, based on their average levels of schooling, discounts obvious differences between schooling credentials obtained before immigration and postimmigration schooling experiences. As suggested later in the analysis, the educational achievement of Black Africans in US schools is actually constrained by barriers associated with their racial minority status, in contrast to what many previous studies suggest. Basing the new model minority thesis on educational differences between Black Africans and US-born Blacks also ignores the fact that such comparisons only tell part of the African immigration story. In particular, it disregards the fact that even before migrating to the United States, Black Africans experienced considerable educational disadvantages relative to Whites in African multiracial societies.

The new model minority thesis is further limited by the fact that it is mainly driven by evidence derived from data on Black African adult immigrants. Focusing on the outcomes of adult immigrants, however, provides limited insight into the achievement patterns of Black African youths. When attention is turned to educational achievement among adolescents, the expected schooling advantage of Black Africans becomes less clear. For example, some comparisons between Black African youths and US-born Blacks suggest that Black Africans have higher achievement outcomes than US-born Blacks (Thomas 2009). Yet Rong and Brown (2001) indicate that Black African adolescents are about as likely to complete high school and four-year colleges as their Caribbean immigrant counterparts. Similarly when the outcomes of immigrant youth from Somalia and Ethiopia are examined, the results indicate that these Black African youths lag behind, in terms of academic performance, compared to students who are Asian or White (Njue and Retish 2010).

Still, the fact that immigrants are considered to be a part of positively selected populations undermines claims to Black African educational exceptionalism. As positively selected populations, immigrants represent the most ambitious, enterprising, and optimistic individuals in their countries of origin. As noted earlier, many Black African immigrants were working professionals in their countries of origin before their departure. Consequently, drawing conclusions about the exceptional ability of Africans, based on comparisons between Africans and US-born Blacks, is problematic. This is because Black African immigrants do not represent the typical Black individual found in Africa. Comparing Black Africans with US-born Blacks, therefore, juxtaposes the outcomes of positively selected Africans with those of all US-born Blacks. When Black immigrants have been compared with other positively selected US-born Blacks (e.g., US-born Black internal migrants) the overall Black immigrant advantage usually disappears (Model 2008). Such findings indicate that when similarly enterprising and ambitious US-born Blacks are compared with Black Africans, it becomes clear that the former can indeed have levels of achievement similar to those of the latter.

Finally, if Black Africans are a new model minority group, we should expect them to have similar or better indicators of educational achievement when compared to White African immigrants. Studies that compare both groups are generally rare. When available, however, they raise serious questions about the validity of the new Black African model minority hypothesis. . For example, in an examination of schooling dropout rates among adolescents, Black Africans were found to be less likely to drop out of school than US-born Blacks; yet the Black African advantage disappears when they are compared with White Africans (Thomas, 2012). In general, therefore, results from such comparisons suggest that it is only when Black African immigrants are compared with a racially different population with a similar migration status that the disadvantages associated with racial minority status begin to emerge.

Disparities in Educational Attainment among Contemporary African Immigrants

In order to better understand educational disparities among contemporary Africans, estimates of educational attainment, conditional on race and Arab-ethnicity, are presented in table 1. These estimates are based on data for adults ages twenty-five and above available in the 2006 to 2008 American Community Survey (ACS). Our first observation from these estimates is that results from the educational comparison between all African immigrants and the US-born are consistent with those reported in previous studies. Thus, by the end of the first decade of the twenty-first century, African immigrants still had higher levels of educational attainment than the US-born population. African immigrants, for example, are more likely to have undergraduate as well as graduate and professional (e.g., nursing and medical) degrees than the US-born. Much of this advantage is driven by the African immigrant population from countries such as Nigeria, South Africa, and Egypt, among whom at least 60 percent had a bachelor's degree or higher.

TABLE 1. HIGHEST LEVEL OF EDUCATIONAL ATTAINMENT AMONG ADULTS ABOVE AGE 24

	LESS THAN HIGH SCHOOL	HIGH-SCHOOL GRADUATES	SOME COLLEGE OR ASSOCIATES	BACHELORS	MASTERS, DOCTORATE, AND PROFESSIONAL
All US-Born	12.2	30.7	29.1	17.6	10.4
All Africans	10.9	18.2	25.7	25.7	19.6
US-Born Blacks	21.5	32.3	29.3	10.8	6.1
Black Non-Arab Africans	12.1	20.3	27.7	22.6	17.3
Black Arab Africans	13.1	21.4	24.2	29.9	11.4
US-Born Whites	11.0	30.7	29.1	18.3	10.9
White Non-Arab Africans	7.1	15.2	25.0	27.3	25.3
White Arab Africans	7.6	13.4	19.8	35.8	23.3

DATA SOURCE: 2006–2008 American Community Survey.

When attention is turned to race and ethnic differences, however, other interesting patterns begin to emerge. For example, despite the lack of research on the educational attainment of Arab and non-Arab Black Africans, table 1 shows that both groups fare relatively well compared to the US-born. For example, Black Arabs and non-Arab Blacks are more likely to have bachelor's or graduate degrees than the US-born. However, at least in terms of graduate-level credentials, non-Arab Black Africans outperform their Black Arab counterparts. Significantly, distinguishing between the outcomes of Arab and non-Arab Blacks does not eliminate the apparent Black African advantage relative to US-born Blacks reported in previous studies. Black Arab Africans, for example, are about three times more likely to achieve up to a bachelor's degree than US-born Blacks. Similarly, compared to US-born Blacks, non-Arab Black Africans are almost three times more likely to have graduate and professional degrees. Surprisingly, however, table 1 also shows that both Black African groups are more likely to have bachelor's or graduate-level degrees than US-born Whites. For example, non-Arab Blacks are more than one and a half times more likely to have graduate and professional credentials than US-born Whites. At the same time, because these differences say nothing about the proportion of Black Africans who received their schooling in the United States, they cannot be used to imply that Black Africans have overcome the racial barriers to achievement within the United States.

Significantly, however, comparisons between Black and White Africans underscore the important association between race and educational attainment found among contemporary African immigrants. Indeed, despite their higher levels of education relative to the US-born, Black Africans, regardless of Arab origin, have lower levels of education than both White African immigrant groups. Unlike Black Africans, for example, at least half of the White Arab and non-Arab White adult populations have a bachelors degree or higher. This White African advantage is more distinct among White Arab than White non-Arab Africans. Black Africans are also more likely than White Africans to be concentrated in the lower levels of educational attainment. For example, Black Africans are more likely to attain only a high-school education than White Africans. Clearly, such differences underscore the fact that there is indeed a schooling disadvantage among Black Africans relative to White African immigrants. However, studies have not determined whether Black-White African schooling differentials are influenced by racial barriers to schooling encountered by Africans after their arrival in the United States.

RACE AND POSTIMMIGRATION EDUCATIONAL ACHIEVEMENT AMONG AFRICANS

After their arrival in the United States, many Black Africans confront new racial conceptions of Blackness and associated barriers to postimmigration achievement. Despite their high overall schooling levels, therefore, Black Africans specifically enrolled in US educational institutions are exposed to structural risks that constrain their achievement levels compared to those of White Africans. Negative perceptions of Arabs in the postimmigration US context may further have adverse implications for educational achievement among Arab immigrants of both races. Such limitations have significant consequences likely to create new patterns of inequality among Africans during the educational incorporation process.

One way to examine the significance of race and Arab ethnicity for postimmigration schooling achievement is to examine the outcomes of African adolescents in US schools. Accordingly, in figure 1, comparative odds ratios are used to examine critical patterns of disparity in educational achievement among high-school-age African youths (i.e., children between ages fifteen and seventeen). The specific outcome of interest is the achievement of adolescents' expected grade for age (see the appendix for methodological details). This measure is an important determinant of schooling progress. As research suggests, adolescents who lag behind in terms of academic progress are usually at a low expected grade for their age and exposed to an elevated risk of dropping out of school (Hauser 1999).

In figure 1, therefore, the gross estimates of the outcomes of African high-school-age youths, regardless of where they started their schooling careers, are presented along with those of their immigrant counterparts who have attended school only in the United States. The latter group is defined as immigrant adolescents who arrived in the United States before age six and therefore started their academic careers in US schools. Within both groups, estimates are also presented for adolescents in four race-ethnic groups, including those for adolescents who racially identify themselves as "other" (e.g., Indian/Asian Africans). Given the fact that these adolescents identify themselves as neither Black nor White, including their outcomes in the analysis is one way to distinguish whether Black Africans experience a unique disadvantage not experienced by other non-White Africans. In general, the principal way in which race and ethnic disparities are assessed is by comparing how members of each group fare in comparison with non-Arab White Africans, the reference group, who have the closest racial and ethnic similarities with US-born non-Hispanic Whites.

FIGURE 1. THE ODDS OF COMPLETING THE EXPECTED GRADE FOR AGE AMONG CHILDREN AGES 15 TO 17, IN COMPARISON TO NON-ARAB WHITES

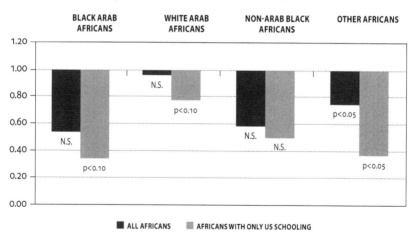

DATA SOURCE: 2006–2008 American Community Survey.

Notes: N.S. means not statistically significant. The dependent variable is the odds of reaching adolescents' expected grade for age. Independent variables: Black Arab Africans, White Arab Africans, Non-Arab Black Africans, Other Africans. Reference group is Non-Arab White Africans.

Comparisons in figure 1 show several patterns that inform our understanding of the relationship between postimmigration educational achievement and racial and ethnic differences among African youths. First, it shows that among all African youths and their counterparts with only US schooling, adolescents in all four race-ethnic groups have lower odds of completing their expected grade for age in than their non-Arab White counterparts. Yet, instructively, the lowest disadvantage relative to non-Arab Whites is found among White Arab adolescents. Apparently, having Arab origins seems to undermine the advantages associated with being White in the American racial context. Second, for all groups, the size of the disadvantage relative to non-Arab Whites is consistently higher among adolescents with only US schooling than among all African adolescents. For example, although all non-Arab Black youths are less likely to achieve their expected grade for age in comparison to all non-Arab White youths, the non-Arab Black disadvantage is considerably higher among adolescents with only US schooling. Associated with this is the fact, as figure 1 shows, that the largest schooling disadvantage, in comparison to non-Arab Whites, is associated with being Black; or more specifically, being Black Arab African. The Black Arab disadvantage is also more distinct in the comparison among children who did all their schooling in the United States. Seemingly, the postmigration US context accelerates racial and ethnic patterns of educational inequality among African youths, and according to these results, non-White Africans, particularly Black Arabs, are more negatively affected by such contextual influences.

What Explains Differences in Postimmigration Educational Achievement among Africans?

During the process of educational incorporation, adolescents with racial and ethnic minority characteristics are exposed to specific constraints that limit their educational achievement patterns compared to those of their counterparts who are White. Although a range of factors is likely to drive these differences, three groups of factors are particularly central to explaining postimmigration schooling inequalities. These include differences in familial socioeconomic attainment, levels of English proficiency, and direct exposure to racial and ethnic prejudice in US schools.

A considerable portion of the achievement differences between Black and White Africans is likely to be explained by familial socioeconomic differentials. As research consistently indicates, high incomes provide access to good-quality schools and increase parents' ability to pay for supplemental services such as tutoring (Gordon, Bridglall, and Meroe 2004; Alderman, Orazem, and Paterno 2001). White African immigrants are more privileged in this regard because, on average, their income levels are higher than those of Black Africans (Kollehlon and Eule 2003). Furthermore, as discussed in chapter 5, there is also considerable variation in wages within race, conditional on Arab ethnic origin, that clearly mirrors the educational disparities found among African adolescents. Based on income differences, therefore, White African adolescents can be expected to have more favorable outcomes than Black African youths since their families have more access to the resources needed to provide them with high-quality schooling.

At the same time, postimmigration educational attainment among African adolescents may also be influenced by differential levels of English proficiency among race-ethnic groups. Evidence from the ACS indicates that Black African high school age youths (79.7 percent) are less likely to be English proficient (i.e., they speak only English or speak English well) than their White counterparts (86.5 percent). However, there is an abundance of evidence linking English proficiency with educational achievement among immigrant youths. For example, students who are English proficient have higher academic expectations than other students and are more likely to progress in school (Hao and Bonstead-Bruns 1998; Thomas 2009). Limited English proficiency, in contrast, is broadly associated with low levels of attainment (Tienda 2011), and the use of languages other than English is negatively associated with immigrant achievement in math and English (Fuligni 1997). It is quite possible, therefore, that language differences among Africans explain some of the educational differences observed after their arrival in the United States.

Multiple regression analysis allows us to examine the extent to which such factors explain postimmigration educational differences conditional on racial and ethnic differences. Again, the example of attainment of the expected grade for age among high-school-age adolescents is used as the main outcome of interest. Figure 2, therefore, presents two sets of bars showing estimated odds ratios from logistic regression analysis of the determinants of postimmigration academic progress. The first set shows unadjusted differences in the odds of achieving the expected grade for age among African adolescents with only US Schooling. These estimates are taken directly from figure 1. The second set shows adjusted estimates that account for differences in family incomes, English proficiency, and demographic (e.g., age and sex) and other factors likely to influence attainment.

FIGURE 2. THE ODDS OF REACHING EXPECTED GRADE FOR AGE AMONG CHILDREN AGES 15 TO 17 WITH ONLY US SCHOOLING, IN COMPARISON TO NON-ARAB WHITES

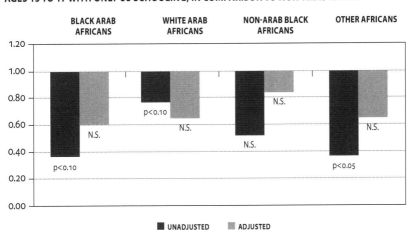

DATA SOURCE: 2006–2008 American Community Survey.
Notes: N.S. means not statistically significant. The dependent variable is the odds of reaching adolescents' expected grade for age. Unadjusted odds account for only the following independent variables: Black Arab Africans, White Arab Africans, Non-Arab Black Africans, Other Africans. Reference group: Non-Arab Whites. Adjusted odds account for these in addition to differences in age, sex, English proficiency, family income (log), year of arrival, and three dummy variables for country of origin–Nigeria, Egypt, and South Africa.

As figure 2 indicates, adjusting for differences in other attributes considerably diminishes the disadvantage of Black, White Arab, and other African youths, in comparison to their non-Arab White counterparts. Accordingly, factors such as English proficiency and family incomes account for a substantial portion of the disadvantage of the majority of African adolescents relative to their non-Arab White counterparts. While the adjusted outcomes of Black, White Arab, and other African youths are not statistically different from that of non-Arab Whites, they nevertheless point to a residual disadvantage among these groups, more so among Black Arabs, compared to non-Arab Whites. Thus, beyond differences in factors such as incomes and English proficiency, other factors may yet account for why immigrants in all four groups have lower levels of achievement than non-Arab White youths.

One possibility is that non-White African youths enrolled in US schools are exposed to classroom environments known to be biased in ways that could negatively affect their academic performance. Among other things, these biases are associated with the fact that US schools generally lack teachers who are themselves members of racial and ethnic minority groups (Bersudskaya and Cataldi 2011). Mounting evidence indicates that the achievement of students from racial and ethnic minority groups is negatively affected by the lack of racial and ethnic diversity among teachers. White teachers, for example, have more negative perceptions of Black than White students (Downey and Pribesh 2004). Yet, more importantly, White African students are more likely to benefit from US classroom contexts than Black Africans because having teachers of the same race significantly increases student test scores (Dee 2004). Studies on the existence of similar biases towards Arab students are generally limited. Nevertheless, available evidence indicates that Arab immigrant youths in US schools experience systematic patterns of oppression, mainly as a result of negative Arab stereotypes, that have negative implications for their schooling experiences (El-Haj 2006). Racial and ethnic biases in US schools are therefore likely to create formidable barriers to academic achievement among Arab-origin and non-White African immigrant youths.

SUMMARY AND IMPLICATIONS

African immigrants clearly have educational attainment patterns that exceed those of the US-born. Indeed, even when educational attainment is decomposed by race and Arab ethnicity, the major African race-ethnic groups still have attainment levels that exceed those of the US-born. These high levels of schooling, however, do not represent typical levels of educational attainment in Africa, where schooling levels are among the world's lowest. Instead, the educational profile of African immigrants largely reflects the fact many of them were highly educated professionals in their origin countries before migration. Declining economic conditions in Africa resulting in the brain drain, and US policy changes, are among the major structural factors responsible for the increasing migration and settlement of highly educated Africans in the United States.

Focusing on the educational differences between African migrants and the US-born, however, understates the degree of racial and ethnic inequality found within the African immigrant population. Furthermore, while Black Africans have higher levels of schooling than US-born Blacks, using such comparisons to suggest that Black Africans have successfully overcome the barrier of racial minority status can be misleading. If Black Africans were unconstrained by racial barriers, they should be expected to have attainment patterns similar to their White African counterparts. Yet when the schooling outcomes of both groups are compared, it becomes clear that the former have systematically lower levels of educational attainment than the latter. African immigrant educational differences are further differentiated by Arab ethnicity. In particular, the evidence indicates that within race, Arab Africans are less likely to have graduate and professional credentials than their non-Arab counterparts. Moreover, when the intersection of race and ethnicity is considered, Black Arab Africans are found to be the least likely African race-ethnic groups to have the highest levels of educational achievement.

Race and Arab ethnicity are also associated with additional barriers to educational achievement among Africans in the postimmigration period. Indeed, among adolescents in US schools, Black Africans are disadvantaged in terms of attainment compared to their White African counterparts. Instructively, this disparity implies that Black Africans experience a less favorable trajectory than White Africans during the educational incorporation process. Part of the postimmigration schooling disadvantage found among Black Africans is driven by barriers associated with their limited familial socioeconomic resources and their comparatively lower levels of English proficiency. Nevertheless, these factors do not fully explain their disadvantage in comparison to their non-Arab White counterparts. Overall, the results indicate that African immigrants with the closest physical similarities with US-born Whites, that is, non-Arab Whites, have the most favorable patterns of educational achievement as they become integrated into society. These immigrants are also the most likely to benefit from teacher-related influences found in the classrooms of US schools.

Racial and ethnic educational inequalities have yet broader implications for the social incorporation of Africans into the United States. Educational attributes, for example, are positively associated with labor force outcomes such as occupational attainment and earnings. Black-White schooling differences among Africans, therefore, suggest that White Africans have a human-capital advantage over Black Africans that predicts greater levels of labor market success among the former than the latter. Apart from human-capital differences, race itself can be a barrier to labor market success that imposes additional constraints on the economic integration of Black Africans. Thus, the dynamics of labor force integration can provide important insights into the ways in which race influences the labor-force incorporation of African immigrants. Occupational issues are thus examined in the next chapter.

.

Occupational Status, Human-Capital Transfer, and the Incorporation Process

An observational study was conducted between January 2006 and June 2007 to investigate reports of race-based employment discrimination at high-end restaurants in New York (Lee 2009). As part of the study, thirty-seven individuals, who were Black, White, Asian, or Latino, were ask to apply for positions as waiters/waitresses advertised by 181 restaurants. The Black applicants included immigrants from Africa and the Caribbean. Regardless of race or immigration status, all applicants were pretrained to ensure that they used similar mannerisms and provided similar answers to questions they were asked after arriving at the restaurants. As expected, the findings from the study were disconcerting; still, they were consistent with research showing how racial and ethnic biases influence hiring decisions. In particular, the results indicated that non-White applicants were about half as likely as White applicants to be offered a job. Furthermore, the work experience of White applicants was less scrutinized than that of Blacks. Surprisingly, White applicants with "foreign" accents were more likely to be hired than other applicants. Yet irrespective of migration status, this apparent "accent" advantage was not observed among Black and other job applicants.

As with these applicants, immigrant racial and ethnic minorities experience occupational disparities that reflect variations in the success of their job-search processes. These variations take on added importance among immigrants because the types of jobs they secure after their arrival have an immediate bearing on their social and economic welfare. Quite apart from their significance for the sustenance of immigrants' families, job-search processes provide immigrants with perhaps their first experience of structured interaction with US institutions. This means that among African immigrants, occupational attainment patterns can be used to draw important conclusions about the ways in which race and ethnicity influence their interactions with these institutions. Variations in the dynamics of occupational attainment also provide initial pointers regarding racial and ethnic disparities in progress towards complete integration into society. As Gordon (1964) argues, the degree to which immigrants are integrated into the institutions of society, for example, employment institutions, is an important indicator of their readiness for more advanced assimilation processes. Thus we can expect that among African immigrant subgroups, trajectories of occupational incorporation will reflect differences in progress towards complete integration into the mainstream of US society.

Also critical to the understanding of African immigrants' occupational in-corporation processes is an examination of their occupational rewards to human capital (e.g., education, language attributes) in the US labor market. Despite consistent evidence showing high levels of schooling among Africans (e.g., Kaba 2007; Kent 2007), however, little is known about the ways in which race and Arab ethnicity affect their occupational rewards to education. For example, scholars are yet to determine whether Black, White, or Arab-origin Africans with similar levels of schooling are equally likely to be employed in prestigious, high-level occupations. Instead, what we know about African experiences in the US labor market comes from selected studies examining income differences in general (e.g., Dodoo 1997; Moore and Amey 2002) and related differences be-tween Black Africans, other Black immigrants, and US-born Blacks (e.g., Butcher 1994; Dodoo 1991). A limited number of studies have also demonstrated that White African immigrants experience greater financial rewards to labor than Black African immigrants (Dodoo and Takyi 2002; Kollehlon and Eule 2003). Within the body of work on African immigrant labor market outcomes, there-fore, a considerable degree of racial and ethnic inequality has been identified.

Labor market rewards such as income and wages can reflect substantial differences in occupational attainment between groups. We know, for example, that doctors, engineers, and scientists typically earn higher incomes than farm laborers and janitors. Yet increasing evidence demonstrates that racial and ethnic minorities are disadvantaged in terms of occupational status compared to Whites, even among the US-born population (Kim and Tamborini 2006; Miech, Eaton, and Liang 2003). Consequently, if Black Africans are found to be occupationally disadvantaged relative to White Africans, this disparity will be consistent with the pattern of labor market differentials observed in previous studies.

Beyond differences in occupational attainment, the extent to which the educational credentials of African immigrants are fully utilized in their current occupations provides an additional perspective on the dynamics of their occupational incorporation processes. In particular, there is now increasing concern among scholars about the occurrence of what is referred to as "brain waste" among highly educated Africans abroad. Brain waste, or the underutilization of human capital, occurs when highly educated individuals work in jobs for which they are overqualified, or have more than the normative level of schooling for their jobs. Examples of this phenomenon appear in the profiles of two African immigrants discussed by Reiter (2010). The first was a Sudanese immigrant who earned a degree in engineering before migrating to the United States. Unable to find a job as an engineer after his arrival, he ended up dealing cards in a local casino. The second immigrant, from Kenya, obtained a degree in architecture before migrating to the United States. Subsequently, he failed to secure a job appropriate for his level training and instead worked as a lower-level construction supervisor. Such highly educated persons who are underemployed will face significant constraints in utilizing their human capital to improve the welfare of their families. However, despite growing evidence on the underutilization of immigrants' human capital, the question of whether "brain waste" occurs differentially among Black and White African immigrants has not been examined in previous studies.

In order to assess whether racial and ethnic minority characteristics are associated with constraints to the utilization of human capital among African immigrants, therefore, three issues need to be determined. First, the specific structural factors that explain why White Africans, especially non-Arab Whites, are expected to be less occupationally disadvantaged than Black African immigrants need to be identified. In other words, we need to address whether there are institutional arrangements, such as employer preferences and accreditation standards, that adversely influence the occupational prospects of Black Africans relative to those of their White African counterparts. Second, the empirical evidence on the occupational outcomes of immigrants in the major African racial and ethnic groups needs to be documented. The third issue is the question of whether racial and ethnic occupational disparities persist even after differences in other attributes (e.g., age, education, language proficiency, and duration of residence) are accounted for.

In the process of addressing these issues, the chapter aims to provide answers to several important questions on the occupational incorporation of African immigrants. What factors contribute to differences in the occupational trajectories of Black and White Africans of Arab and non-Arab origins? What happens to racial and ethnic differences in occupational attainment as duration of residence increases? Do highly educated Africans with racial and ethnic minority characteristics receive lower occupational rewards to schooling than non-Arab White Africans? Answers to these questions will be useful for developing a clearer portrait of the scale and determinants of occupational inequality among African immigrants during the incorporation process.

RACE AND THE HIRING PREFERENCES OF EMPLOYERS

One reason for expecting White African immigrants to have more favorable occupational trajectories than their Black counterparts is found in the queuing perspective on job-search processes in the US labor market. According to this perspective, employers faced with the decision of hiring potential employees create an imaginary queue based on their subjective rankings of qualified employees. Accordingly, the most desirable employees are placed at the top of the queue and the least qualified at the bottom. In the US labor market context, the social construction of race is a significant determinant of where workers are placed in these rankings. For example, Model (1997) suggests that in terms of general preferences, Whites and Blacks are respectively the most and least preferred employees. There is also evidence consistent with the notion that employers' subjective rankings reflect racial preferences and the influence of negative racial stereotypes. Moss and Tilly (1995), for example, suggest that US employers believe that Black men lack the motivation to work, unlike non-Black men, and that Black men with low levels of schooling are particularly likely to be considered hostile and intimidating. In a more recent study by both authors, they further maintain that negative stereotypes about racial minorities are particularly high among employers of blue-collar workers (Moss and Tilly 2003).

Limited studies are available on the relative placement of Arab workers within employers' subjective rankings. Bushman and Bonacci (2004) argue that since the events of September 11, 2001, considerable increases have been observed in work-related discrimination against Arabs in the United States. Although they do not differentiate between Arab immigrants by race, their argument suggests that at least in comparison to their non-Hispanic White counterparts, Arab-origin employees are less preferred. Significantly, Bushman and Bonacci found a drop in earnings among Arabs, relative to those of non-Hispanic Whites, in the immediate period following the terrorist attacks in September

2001. Yet their analysis indicates that the decline did not apply to the outcomes of African Arabs. They interpret this as implying that employment discrimination among Arabs is mostly targeted towards Arabs from countries in the Middle East that have been associated with terrorist attacks. Other scholars, however, argue that terrorism-related stereotypes do not necessarily form the sole basis of employment-related discrimination against Arabs. Naber (2000), for example, suggests that the low preference for Arab workers may also be driven by discrimination based on their presumed political views, religion, and appearance. These Arab-related biases generally predate the events of September 11, 2001.

Studies on the significance of immigrants' race and ethnicity in labor force incorporation processes have produced a number of findings consistent with queuing perspectives. Lieberson (1981), for example, suggests that employment differences between European immigrants and Blacks in the early part of the twentieth century were driven by employers' subjective rankings used in queuing-related processes. Reports consistent with a specific Black African disadvantage, in terms of employer preferences, have also emerged in recent studies. For example, Frosch (2010) describes incidences of unequal treatment of African workers, relative to their White and Hispanic counterparts, that were driven by employers' stated preferences for the types of faces they would like to see working in their institutions.

Given employers' presumed preference for non-Black workers, some scholars (e.g., Model 1997) have suggested that the presence of Blacks in the labor market benefits all employees with other racial characteristics. By implication, therefore, Black Africans are expected to be less preferred than White Arab Africans. Indeed, some of the available evidence is consistent with the hypothesis that Black workers are generally less preferred by employers compared to workers in predominantly non-Black Arab immigrant groups. In particular, Charara (2000) maintains that in the early years of the twentieth century, US-born Blacks were systematically excluded from jobs in Detroit's motor industry at a time when a significant portion of the industry's employees were Arab immigrants.

Employer hiring preferences can therefore affect racial and ethnic differences in occupational incorporation among Africans in a number of ways. Based on the presumed racial preferences of employers, non-Arab White Africans, on average, are expected to have higher levels of occupational attainment than other African immigrants. Similarly, non-Arab Whites are also expected to be the most likely African immigrants to have jobs that match their levels of schooling. In addition, they are expected to be the least likely to be overqualified or have more than the normative schooling level associated with their jobs. Given the negative influence of Arab stereotypes, however, Arab Africans are expected to have less favorable occupational trajectories than non-Arabs within each race. At the same time, the primacy of race as a determinant of occupational outcomes is expected to be underscored by the fact that although White Arabs will have less favorable outcomes than non-Arab Whites, they will still outperform Black Africans of Arab and non-Arab origins. Black Africans, regardless of ethnic origin, are thus expected to have higher levels of brain waste, or have more than the expected level of schooling associated with their jobs, compared to White African immigrants.

The Transferability of Human Capital among Immigrants

Another determining factor that affects the occupational rewards received by immigrants is the extent to which their human-capital endowments are consistent with those desired by US employers. Unfortunately, human capital acquired before migration is not always recognized in immigrants' destination countries because attributes such as education, skills, and linguistic characteristics are not easily transferable across countries. Limited transferability of human capital can thus negatively influence the occupational outcomes of immigrants, and these adverse implications are well documented in several studies. For example, Chiswick and Miller (2010) demonstrate that preimmigration work experience is related to less favorable employment outcomes. In other words, immigrants typically receive suboptimal rewards for work experience acquired before migration. Findings reported by Mattoo, Neagu, and Ozden (2008) also indicate that poorly transferable skills among immigrants increase their risks of underplacement in the labor market. In contrast to immigrants with foreign human capital, immigrants who acquire human-capital credentials after arrival in their destination countries tend to have more favorable labor force outcomes. As demonstrated by Bratsberg and Ragan (2002), immigrants with schooling acquired in the United States typically receive higher wages than their counterparts with schooling acquired before migration.

Notwithstanding the well-recognized constraints to human-capital transferability among immigrants, the extent to which they account for racial and ethnic occupational disparities among African immigrants has not been investigated. Yet, in general, the influence of these constraints on such disparities can be transmitted through a number of channels. Akresh (2006), for example, argues that human-capital transferability is greater among immigrants from countries that are culturally similar to the United States. One implication of this argument is that Arab Africans, who predominantly originate from societies that are culturally dissimilar to the United States, experience greater occupational disadvantages than non-Arab White Africans, who mainly come from South Africa. Levels of economic development in origin countries also increase the likelihood that education provided in these countries will reflect the latest developments in technology required in labor markets abroad (de Oliveiria, Santos, and Kiker 2000). Here again, the main implication is that the high levels of development found in the major origin countries of non-Arab White Africans (e.g., South Africa and Namibia) will contribute to the increased transferability of their education credentials compared to the credentials of, for example, Black Africans.

Related to the economic development hypothesis is the fact that employers in Western countries are generally unwilling to accept licensing and accreditation requirements from less developed countries (Boyd and Thomas 2002; Reitz 2001). Medical graduates from poor African countries, for example, are unlikely to be employed as doctors upon their arrival in the United States, because their credentials are not always recognized by medical employers. By contrast, evidence indicates that graduates in Africa's wealthier countries, for example, South Africa, are actively recruited for jobs suited for their levels of schooling in highly industrialized Western countries, including the United States (Crush 2002; Hagopian et al. 2004). At least with regard to medical graduates, scholars (e.g., Hagopian et al. 2004) further suggest that US employer preferences for South African immigrants is in part driven by strong curricular similarities between the two countries. In summary, because Black African immigrants are more likely than White Africans to originate from poor African countries, the economic development perspective will predict that they will be more likely to be overeducated, or experience brain waste, than White African immigrants.

Beyond the advantage associated with originating from more developed countries, group differences in duration of residence can also result in racial occupational differences through their indirect influence on the acquisition of US credentials. Accordingly, racial groups with a longer history of legally authorized immigration to the United States, such as White Africans, are more likely to have obtained US educational credentials than more recent immigrant groups. Black Africans, unlike their White counterparts, are also disadvantaged in this regard, due to their comparatively longer history of legal exclusion from the United States (Gordon 1998; Kent 2007).

Language as a form of human capital also varies in terms of its transferability across countries in ways that have important implications for racial and ethnic occupational inequalities among Africans. Linguistically, the origin countries of non-Arab White Africans are more similar to the United States than most origin countries of Black or Arab-origin Africans. In other words, English is spoken in a greater proportion of the origin countries of non-Arab White Africans than in those with Africa's predominantly Arab populations. As consistently demonstrated in prior studies (Chiswick and Miller 2002; Dávila and Mora 2004), high levels of English-language proficiency play a significant role in increasing the likelihood of occupational and labor market success among immigrants. Collectively, therefore, non-Arab Whites, as a result of their high levels of premigration exposure to English, are likely to have a further advantage compared to other Africans. Moreover, this advantage is likely to manifest itself in the form of high levels of occupational attainment.

THE OCCUPATIONAL ATTAINMENT PATTERNS OF AFRICAN IMMIGRANTS

Data available in the American Community Survey (ACS) are useful for examining whether the empirical evidence on occupational patterns is consistent with the propositions and conceptual explanations found in existing studies. Racial and ethnic differences in occupational attainment of Africans can be described using a number of measures found in these data. One of these, the Socioeconomic Index (SEI), was originally developed by Duncan (1961) and more recently updated by Hauser and Warren (1997). Under this schema, individuals with more prestigious occupations, such as medical doctors and engineers, typically have higher SEI scores, while those in comparatively lower-level occupations, for example, janitors and bus drivers, receive lower scores. Although there is a lack of comprehensive information on African immigrant occupations in many US surveys, this information, including SEI scores, is available in the ACS.

To get an initial sense of broad racial and ethnic differences in occupational incorporation, we start by examining differences in SEI scores among Africans, based on race and Arab ethnicity. To do this, we focus on the outcomes of working-age adults between the ages of twenty-five and sixty-four. As figure 3 indicates, there are different patterns of occupational incorporation among African across racial and ethnic lines. For example, there is a clear occupational advantage, as measured by SEI scores, among White Arabs and non-Arab Whites compared to all Black Africans. In other words, immigrants in the two White African groups are more likely to hold prestigious occupations than are Black African immigrants. Non-Arab Whites and Black Arabs have the most and least favorable occupational outcomes, as their respective indices are the highest and lowest among the groups. The initial evidence shown in figure 3 also supports the notion that Arab ethnicity is associated with an occupational disadvantage within race. Notwithstanding the Arab disadvantage within the population of White Africans, however, White Arabs, on average, are more likely to hold prestigious jobs than non-Arab Africans who are Black. In line with expectations, therefore, the indices suggest that Black Africans have unique occupational experiences and that these experiences are broadly characterized by a considerable degree of occupational disadvantage.

FIGURE 3. OCCUPATIONAL STATUS INDICES OF BLACK AND WHITE AFRICANS

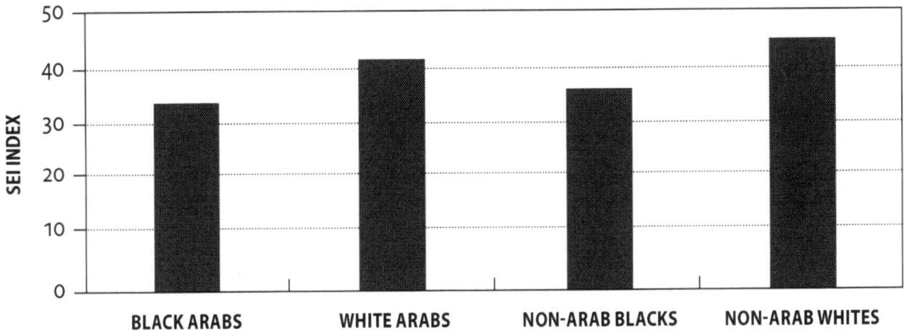

DATA SOURCE: 2006–2008 American Community Survey.

Further clarity is brought to the issue of whether increasing exposure to the United States is associated with differential occupational returns among African immigrant race-ethnic groups. Accordingly, figure 4 addresses two questions. First, is increasing duration of US residence associated with consistent increases in occupational status across all African race-ethnic groups? Second, how do racial and ethnic occupational differences among recent immigrants compare with those found among longer-term immigrants?

With regard to the first question, figure 4 shows that, indeed, Africans who have longer years of US residence typically have higher levels of occupational attainment than their more recent counterparts. Recent African immigrants, including those who have lived in the United States for less than ten years, seemingly have less well-developed job-search networks that can facilitate occupational mobility than do Africans with more than thirty years of US residence. A clear exception to these trends, however, is found among non-Arab Whites. Specifically, figure 4 shows negligible increases in occupational status across all non-Arab White duration-of-residence cohorts. This limited increase across time seems to be driven by their high levels of occupational prestige, even among more recent immigrants. In all duration-of-residence cohorts conversely, there is considerable racial stratification in occupational attainment. As expected, White Africans consistently outperform Black Africans, regardless of duration of residence. Within race, ethnically stratified occupational attainment patterns are underscored by the consistent Arab African disadvantage in comparison to non-Arabs.

As for the question of how racial and ethnic occupational disparities compare among recent and longer-term immigrants, figure 4 shows that although there are larger inequalities among the former, occupational outcomes slightly converge among the latter. As the trends thus suggest, the comparative advantage of non-Arab Whites is systematically lower among immigrants with longer years of residence. Duration of residence is thus somewhat associated with a slight decline in the disadvantage of Black Africans and White Arab Africans relative to non-Arab Whites. Instructively, however, the only group that achieves complete occupational convergence with non-Arab Whites is the White Arab group. This finding suggests that long-term White Arab immigrants are more able to overcome the occupational disadvantages associated with ethnic minority characteristics. Finally, as shown in figure 4, both groups of Black Africans remain consistently disadvantaged relative to non-Arab White Africans in all duration-of-residence cohorts.

FIGURE 4. OCCUPATIONAL ATTAINMENT BY DURATION OF RESIDENCE

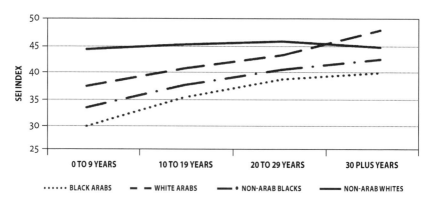

DATA SOURCE: 2006–2008 American Community Survey.

AFRICANS IN WHITE- AND BLUE-COLLAR OCCUPATIONS

Occupational attainment patterns can also be understood by examining inequalities at the top and bottom of the occupational spectrum. Stratification patterns within white- and blue-collar occupations can thus provide an additional perspective on the dynamics of African immigrants' occupational incorporation processes. In figures 5 and 6, therefore, attention is turned to the question of whether disparities exist in the distribution of Africans in blue- and white-collar occupations respectively.

Blue-collar occupations generally serve a strategic purpose to immigrants during the socioeconomic incorporation process. Such jobs are typically utilized to provide temporary sustenance while immigrants acquire country-level capital needed for subsequent occupational mobility. With increasing duration of residence, therefore, immigrants tend to leave these jobs for more prestigious, white-collar occupations (Akresh 2008). As figure 5 indicates, however, Black African immigrants are considerably more likely to hold blue-collar jobs than White African immigrants. Moreover, Black Africans seem less able than White Arab Africans to move from blue-collar to relatively more prestigious jobs as duration of residence increases. For example, although the percentage employed in blue-collar jobs tends to decrease with increasing duration of residence among Black Arab and White Arab Africans, the decreases are more consistent among the latter than among the former. Furthermore, figure 5 shows that the prevalence of blue-collar jobs among White Arabs and non-Arab Blacks with less than ten years of residence is generally similar. However, among immigrants with about thirty years of residence, non-Arab Blacks are three times more likely than White Arabs to hold such jobs, suggesting that the former have fewer opportunities to move to higher-level jobs than the latter have. As expected, non-Arab Whites are the least likely to be employed in blue-collar occupations, and their considerable underrepresentation in these occupations is consistent with the fact that, on average, they have the highest levels of occupational attainment.

Corresponding distributions for Africans employed in white-collar occupations are presented in figure 6, and as in figure 5, they underscore the consistently more favorable occupational attainment patterns of non-Arab Whites compared to other Africans. For example, more than half of all non-Arab Whites hold white-collar occupations in all duration-of-residence cohorts. In contrast, there is a consistent disadvantage associated with racial minority status, especially among Black African Arabs, who are considerably less likely have such occupations. Unlike White and non-Arab Black Africans, Black Arabs

FIGURE 5. PERCENTAGE OF AFRICANS WITH BLUE-COLLAR OCCUPATIONS BY DURATION OF RESIDENCE

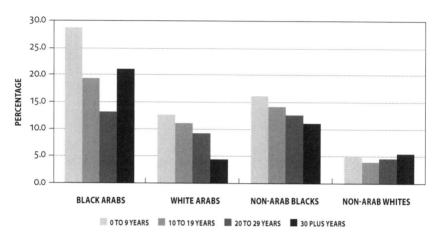

FIGURE 6. PERCENTAGE OF AFRICANS WITH WHITE-COLLAR OCCUPATIONS BY DURATION OF RESIDENCE

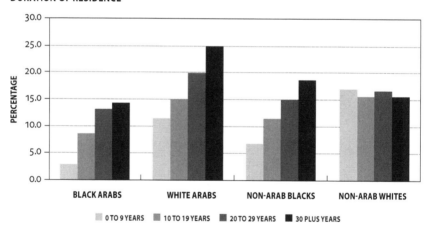

DATA SOURCE: 2006–2008 American Community Survey.
Note: Consistent with other scholars (e.g. Alderman and Tolnay 2003; Rumbaut 1995), white-collar occupations are those occupations classified under the "Professional and Technical" and "Managers, Officials, and Proprietors" categories by the US Census Bureau. These occupations include physicians, dentists, engineers, and chief executives.

also do not experience substantial increases in their likelihood of having white-collar occupations beyond their twenty-ninth year of residence. In comparison, among White Arabs, the results show a consistent increase in their likelihood of obtaining white-collar occupations with increasing duration of US residence. This may partly explain why White Arab Africans outperform non-Arab White Africans among immigrants with the longest years of US residence.

Occupational Differences among Foreign- and US-Educated African Graduates

We now turn our attention to the question of whether occupational inequalities among Africans are associated with differences in the international transferability of educational credentials. As noted earlier, foreign-educated immigrants from developed countries with education systems similar to those in the West tend to have better labor force outcomes than their counterparts from countries with less-developed systems. Since the predominant origin countries of non-Arab White Africans are the more developed countries in Africa, however, it is analytically necessary to separate the influences of race from that of origin contexts in investigating what drives their occupational successes. If the non-Arab White advantage is driven only by a more-developed origin context, and not by race, the comparative occupational advantage should disappear when the occupational patterns of US-educated immigrants are examined.

Table 2, therefore, compares the SEI scores of Black and White Africans, of Arab and non-Arab origin, who have US and foreign university credentials. More information on the ways in which these credentials are identified is available in the appendix. Overall, three major findings are presented in the table. First, and not surprisingly, the non-Arab White occupational advantage relative to other Africans is greater among immigrants with foreign rather than US education credentials. In other words, the empirical evidence is consistent with the notion that the foreign credentials of non-Arab White Africans are more useful for achieving occupational mobility in the United States than the credentials of other foreign-educated Africans. Second, table 2 shows that although non-Arab Whites with foreign credentials do as well, in terms of SEI scores, as their counterparts with US educational credentials, the SEI scores among non-Arab Blacks are considerably lower among foreign- than among US-educated immigrants. Foreign-educated non-Arab Blacks, in other words, experience a substantial occupational penalty, but foreign-educated non-Arab Whites do not. Occupational disadvantages associated with the possession of foreign credentials are also found among Black Arabs and White Arabs. Yet, in relative terms, the disadvantage is greater among the former than among the latter. A third finding shown in the table is that foreign-educated Black Arabs have the lowest levels of occupational attainment among foreign-educated Africans. Seemingly, these immigrants are disadvantaged on three dimensions; they are foreign-educated, racially Black, and of Arab ethnic origin.

TABLE 2. SEI INDICES FOR FOREIGN AND US GRADUATES BY ETHNICITY AND TIMING OF ARRIVAL

	BLACK ARABS	WHITE ARABS	NON-ARAB BLACKS	NON-ARAB WHITES
US-educated graduates				
All	44.7	52.4	49.8	52.0
0 to 9 years	44.9	48.7	49.5	51.2
10 to 19 years	39.6	51.4	49.7	51.7
20 to 29 years	49.9	52.1	50.0	52.6
30-plus years	47.2	54.8	50.0	51.9
Foreign-educated graduates				
All	41.0	45.4	45.4	51.7
0 to 9 years	38.7	43.3	42.4	51.4
10 to 19 years	42.2	46.4	48.4	51.6
20 to 29 years	45.3	45.9	47.5	51.8
30-plus years	53.1	50.0	44.4	54.3

DATA SOURCE: 2006–2008 American Community Survey.

Among US-educated Africans, non-Arab Whites, on average, continue to have higher levels of occupational attainment than Arab and non-Arab Blacks. Interestingly, however, the disparity between non-Arab Whites and White Arabs disappears among this group of graduates. The lower average level of occupational attainment found among Arab, as opposed to non-Arab, Whites in figure 3 is probably a consequence of the limited transferability of credentials obtained by White Arab Africans before migration to the United States. When this barrier is eliminated among US-educated graduates, both groups do about equally well in terms of their occupational prestige. Table 2 even suggests that the gains associated with having US credentials are greater among White Arabs than non-Arabs among immigrants with at least thirty years of US residence.

For Black Africans, a consistent occupational disadvantage is again observed relative to White Africans, one that is seemingly unexplained by the apparent limited acceptability of foreign education credentials. Rather, even among US-educated graduates, Black Africans, especially Black Arabs, remain occupationally disadvantaged relative to their White African counterparts. Furthermore, among US-educated graduates with the longest years of residence, Black Africans, unlike White Arabs, do not achieve occupational parity with their counterparts who are non-Arab White.

EXPLAINING RACIAL AND ETHNIC DISPARITIES IN OCCUPATIONAL ATTAINMENT

To what extent do differences in factors such as age, sex, country of origin, duration of residence, and language proficiency collectively account for racial and ethnic occupational differences among African immigrants? This question is answered using results from simple multiple regression analyses. These results are first presented for the analysis examining overall racial and ethnic occupational disparities, following which those examining the determinants of disparities among foreign- and US-educated graduates are presented.

Figure 7 presents results from the analysis of overall disparities among Africans and continues to show significant patterns of occupational disadvantage in comparison to White Africans (the reference group). If these disadvantages were absent, the coefficients for all groups shown in the figure would move upwards and would be equal to zero. Also included in the figure is the small group of "other" African immigrants, that is, non-Black and non-White Africans. As the results show, when occupational disparities are adjusted to account for age and sex differences (i.e., in the first set of bars), White Arabs, as well as all Black Africans, still have lower levels of occupational attainment than non-Arab Whites. Similarly, age and sex differences do not explain why White Arabs have a lower comparative disadvantage than Black Arabs and non-Arab Blacks. Figure 7 also underscores the extreme degree of occupational disadvantage associated with having Black racial characteristics. In short, it demonstrates that both groups of Black Africans do less well even in comparison to "other" Africans who are neither Black nor White.

The second set of bars presents results of adjusted occupational differences that further account for the influence of factors such as differences in country of origin, English proficiency, work experience, duration of residence, and US

FIGURE 7. GENERAL ADJUSTED DIFFERENCES IN OCCUPATIONAL STATUS INDEX IN COMPARISON TO NON-ARAB WHITE AFRICANS

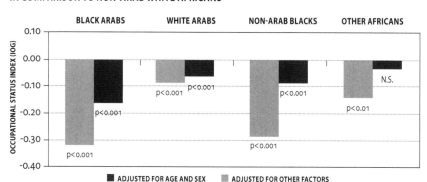

DATA SOURCE: 2006-2008 American Community Survey.
Notes: N.S. means not statistically significant. The dependent variable is the log of the SEI index. Racial and ethnic coefficients adjusted for age and sex are derived from models also controlling for age and sex. Racial and ethnic coefficients adjusted other for factors also include controls for age and sex as well as the following independent variables: English proficiency, work experience, three dummy variables for country of origin – Nigeria, Egypt, and South Africa, and US citizenship status.

citizenship status. Accounting for these influences considerably reduces the occupational disadvantage of each group, relative to non-Arab Whites. The reductions also tend to be largest among Black Arabs and therefore suggest that factors such as low levels of English proficiency among these immigrants may partly explain why they are occupationally disadvantaged compared to non-Arab Whites. According to the 2003–2008 ACS data, for example, 69 percent of White Arabs and 53 percent of Black Arabs were proficient in English; that is, they spoke English very well or spoke only English. In contrast, the corresponding figure among non-Arab Whites was 92 percent. Significantly, however, the occupational disadvantage of both Black African groups persists even after accounting for the influence of other additional factors, while that for "other" Africans is no longer statistically significant. This persistent Black African immigrant disadvantage, therefore, suggests that their suboptimal occupational attainment levels are not explained by factors such as the economic context of their origin countries, duration of residence, or English proficiency.

Figures 8 and 9 respectively extend the examination of the determinants of racial and ethnic occupational inequalities to the outcomes of foreign- and US-educated graduates. In general, they show that accounting for age and sex differences eliminates neither the racial and ethnic occupational disparities found among Africans with foreign education (figure 8), nor those found among Africans with US schooling (figure 9). Results in the second set of bars in figure

8 also suggest that factors such differences in English proficiency, duration of residence, and country of origin do not explain why White Arabs and Black Africans are occupationally disadvantaged among foreign-educated graduates. Furthermore, figure 8 shows that the lower White Arab disadvantage compared to non-Arab Blacks among foreign-educated Africans disappears after accounting for the influence of other factors. In comparison, Black Africans remain the

FIGURE 8. FOREIGN-EDUCATION GRADUATES: ADJUSTED DIFFERENCES IN OCCUPATIONAL STATUS IN COMPARISON TO NON-ARAB WHITE AFRICANS

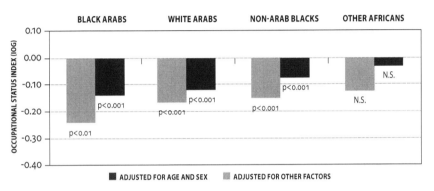

FIGURE 9. US-EDUCATED GRADUATES: ADJUSTED DIFFERENCES IN OCCUPATIONAL STATUS IN COMPARISON TO NON-ARAB WHITE AFRICANS

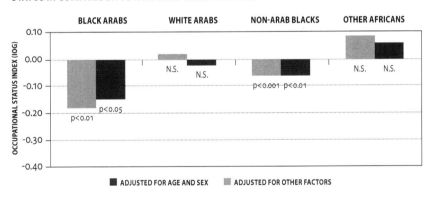

DATA SOURCE: 2006-2008 American Community Survey.
Notes: N.S. means not statistically significant. The dependent variable is the log of the SEI index among US-educated graduates. Racial and ethnic coefficients adjusted for age and sex are derived from models also controlling for age and sex. Racial and ethnic coefficients adjusted for other factors also include controls for age and sex as well as the following independent variables: English proficiency, work experience, three dummy variables for country of origin – Nigeria, Egypt, and South Africa, and US citizenship status.

most distinctively disadvantaged group among US-educated graduates even after adjusting for other factors (figure 9). Both sets of findings reinforce the argument that Black African graduates are occupationally disadvantaged compared to their non-Black African peers, regardless of whether the comparisons are based on where schooling credentials are obtained.

RACE, ETHNICITY, AND THE UTILIZATION OF SCHOOLING CREDENTIALS

Another perspective on the occupational incorporation of African immigrants is provided by the examination of the extent to which their educational credentials are appropriately utilized in their current occupations. Previous studies, such as Duncan and Hoffman (1981) and Vaisey (2006), have identified three education-occupation matching possibilities essential for understanding the utilization of schooling in the labor market. First, employees can ideally have the appropriate level of schooling, or be correctly matched, with their jobs. Second, they may have more than the normative schooling expectations, or be overeducated, for their jobs. Third, they may have less than the normative schooling requirements, or be undereducated for their jobs.

An initial picture of the prevalence of education-occupation mismatches among African immigrants is presented in table 3. Most of the education-occupation matching patterns shown in the table are consistent with expectations. For example, a higher percentage of non-Arab Whites than of other Africans have jobs that are correctly matched with their level of schooling. Non-Arab Whites also seem to have a slight advantage over most groups in terms of undereducation, and they are clearly the least likely to be overeducated for their jobs. Surprisingly, non-Arab Blacks are more likely to be undereducated for their jobs than White Arab Africans. This disparity, however, disappears among immigrants with the longest years of US residence. Also surprising is the fact that regardless of race, Arab Africans generally have the highest rates of overeducation among African immigrants.

A number of implications can be derived from these findings. First, if undereducation disparities reflect employer racial preferences, the results would suggest that, at least in terms of having jobs for which immigrants are underqualified, non-Arab Whites *and* non-Arab Blacks are preferred to Arab-origin Africans. Second, the high prevalence of overeducation among Arab Africans indicates that they are least able among Africans to fully utilize their schooling in the US labor market. In other words, Arab African immigrants have the highest levels of the brain waste. Third, the Arab overeducation disadvantage is mainly driven by the outcomes of recent immigrants. Among immigrants with at least thirty-years of residence, for example, Arab Africans are considerably more likely to be correctly matched or even undereducated for their jobs than non-Arab Blacks.

TABLE 3. PERCENTAGE DISTRIBUTION OF AFRICAN IMMIGRANTS WHO ARE OVEREDUCATED, UNDEREDUCATED, OR CORRECTLY MATCHED FOR THEIR JOBS

	BLACK ARABS	WHITE ARABS	NON-ARAB BLACKS	NON-ARAB WHITES
Undereducated				
All	18.0	15.4	20.2	21.2
Duration of residence				
0 to 9 years	21.7	17.3	22.0	22.9
10 to 19 years	12.8	13.2	20.7	21.5
20 to 29 years	16.0	12.9	17.9	18.7
30-plus years	15.8	19.5	14.8	21.4
Correctly matched				
All	35.0	34.2	33.9	38.2
Duration of residence				
0 to 9 years	30.8	30.8	33.5	36.8
10 to 19 years	36.1	34.6	34.8	40.7
20 to 29 years	46.0	36.5	34.3	39.4
30-plus years	47.4	37.0	31.2	36.6
Over-Educated				
All	47.0	50.4	45.9	40.7
Duration of residence				
0 to 9 years	47.5	51.9	44.5	40.3
10 to 19 years	51.1	52.2	44.5	37.8
20 to 29 years	38.0	50.6	47.8	41.9
30-plus years	36.8	43.4	54.1	42.0

DATA SOURCE: 2006–2008 American Community Survey.

A general sense of the extent to which factors such as English proficiency, US citizenship status, and having foreign rather than US university-level credentials are associated with racial disparities in education-occupation matching is provided in table 4. These estimates show predicted probabilities of overeducation, undereducation, and correct matches based on a number of immigrant attributes. A simple way to interpret these estimates is as follows; predicted probabilities range from 0 to 1 with larger estimates reflecting a greater likelihood of observing the respective outcome. Accordingly, because non-Arab Whites generally have higher predicted estimates of undereducation and correct matches, the results demonstrate that they hold a clear and consistent matching advantage relative to Africans with similar linguistic, citizenship, and other characteristics.

TABLE 4. PREDICTED PROBABILITIES OF OVEREDUCATION, UNDEREDUCATION, AND CORRECT MATCHES AMONG AFRICAN IMMIGRANTS

	OVEREDUCATION	CORRECT MATCH	UNDEREDUCATION
English Proficient			
White Arabs	0.50	0.36	0.14
Black Arabs	0.51	0.36	0.12
Non-Arab Blacks	0.50	0.34	0.16
Non-Arab Whites	0.41	0.20	0.39
Naturalized citizens			
White Arabs	0.51	0.35	0.14
Black Arabs	0.43	0.45	0.12
Non-Arab Blacks	0.47	0.35	0.18
Non-Arab Whites	0.39	0.41	0.20
Foreign-educated graduates			
White Arabs	0.59	0.36	0.05
Black Arabs	0.67	0.30	0.03
Non-Arab Blacks	0.61	0.34	0.05
Non-Arab Whites	0.44	0.52	0.04
US-educated graduates			
White Arabs	0.53	0.45	0.02
Black Arabs	0.60	0.40	0.00
Non-Arab Blacks	0.57	0.39	0.04
Non-Arab Whites	0.48	0.47	0.05

Notes: For each of these four attributes, i.e., English proficiency, US citizenship status, etc., predicted probabilities are derived from separate multinomial regression models estimating whether they are associated with mismatch statuses in each race-ethnic group. Thus, the predicted probabilities in the table are derived from a total of sixteen separate multinomial regression models, each of which also controls for age, age-squared, and sex.

Among immigrants who are English proficient, the probability of undereducation among non-Arab Whites is at least twice as high as among Africans in the other groups. Thus, among Africans who are English proficient, non-Arab Whites are the most likely to be underqualified or have less than the normative schooling expectations for their jobs. Interestingly, a similar undereducation advantage is not observed among English-proficient White-Arabs. Non-Arab White African proficient English speakers also seem better able to avoid overeducation than White Arabs and all Black Africans. Among Africans who are US citizens, non-Arab Whites also have the highest and lowest probabilities of undereducation and overeducation respectively. Surprisingly, citizenship status is also associated with a higher probability of having correct matches between job and education among Black Arabs, although the reasons for this are generally unclear.

As with the overall patterns of educational attainment, overeducation among Arab Africans seems driven by the limited transferability of their schooling credentials. Consequently, they are more likely to be overeducated than other Africans among foreign-educated graduates. In contrast, foreign-educated non-Arab Whites are considerably more likely to have occupations that are correctly matched with their schooling. Regardless of race or ethnicity, however, US-educated Africans have higher probabilities of being correctly matched with their jobs than foreign-educated Africans, although non-Arab Whites are an exception to this pattern. Among US-educated graduates, however, Black Arabs and non-Arab Blacks still have worse overeducation outcomes than their counterparts who are non-Arab White.

SUMMARY AND IMPLICATIONS

While occupational incorporation processes play an important role in the labor-force integration of immigrants, significant differences exist in the actual experiences of African immigrants. Not surprisingly, racial differences are important influences of these differences. Moreover, African immigrants experience diverse prospects of occupational incorporation based on the intersection of race and Arab ethnicity. These racial and ethnic differences are reflected not only in overall levels of occupational attainment but also in the extent to which African immigrants are able to secure jobs that match their completed level of schooling.

Consistent with queuing perspectives, the most favorable occupational outcomes are found among African immigrants with racial characteristics similar to those of the non-Hispanic White US population. Accordingly, the most favorable pathways of occupational incorporation are found among non-Arab White Africans. These immigrants are the most likely to hold white-collar occupations and the least likely to have more education than the normative schooling expectations of their occupations. Non-Arab Whites thus have the lowest prevalence of brain waste among Africans. In part, their overall occupational advantage seems driven by the high level of transferability of schooling credentials they obtained from their countries of origin. Nevertheless, they also have more favorable occupational outcomes, such as higher levels of occupational prestige and undereducation, than other Africans, even among US-educated graduates. The non-Arab White advantage further extends to the outcomes of African immigrants who are naturalized citizens, and to those who speak English proficiently. Instructively, therefore, the persistence of the non-Arab White occupational advantage indicates that they would still have the most favorable occupation outcomes even in the absence of differences in acculturation or in the transferability of human capital. Non-Arab Whites are thus better positioned than other Africans to translate civic, linguistic, and human-capital gains during the incorporation process into occupational mobility in the US labor market. Among White Africans, however, the degree of occupational advantage relative to Black Africans is lower among White Arabs. At least in terms of overall occupational prestige, foreign-educated White Arab graduates do not necessarily outperform their counterparts who are non-Arab Black.

Occupational inequalities among Africans further support the argument that race is a significant barrier to the occupational incorporation of Black African immigrants. In line with this argument, Black Africans face occupational disadvantages among both US- and foreign-educated Africans and are typically more likely to be employed in blue-collar jobs than White Africans. In terms of overall occupational attainment patterns, the results show that the Black disadvantage is even greater among foreign-educated than among US-educated Africans. Thus, the limited transferability of schooling credentials obtained before migrating to the United States compounds the disadvantage of racial minority status faced by foreign-educated Blacks.

Notably, however, there is a clear distinction between the occupational outcomes of Black Arabs and non-Arab Blacks. In particular, the Black disadvantage is consistently greater among the former than the latter. Black Arabs, therefore, experience a double disadvantage as a result of both their racial minority status and their Arab ethnic characteristics. The combination of these factors also exposes them to unique types of discrimination that constrict their prospects for occupational mobility. Indeed, Aynte (2007) suggests that some Black Africans from Arab-related backgrounds experience high levels of job discrimination on the basis of their religion even from US-born Black employers.

Tellingly, the analysis provides no basis for concluding that occupational disparities between Black and White Africans will converge during the incorporation process. Among more incorporated long-term migrants, for example, occupational attainment levels are considerably higher among White than among Black African immigrants. These disparate occupational incorporation patterns are likely to have significant implications for the social integration of African immigrants. Gordon's theoretical arguments suggest that the less favorable incorporation of Black Africans into US employment institutions will make them less prepared than White Africans for more advanced social processes such as intermarriage. A more immediate implication of these occupation disparities, is that they will result in racial and ethnic inequalities in income. These inequalities are important for providing a more comprehensive picture of the economic incorporation processes of African immigrants. As a result, their dynamics and determinants are systematically examined in the following chapter.

Earnings, Self-Employment, and Economic Incorporation

W hile the occupational outcomes of Africans help us understand the dynamics of their integration into the labor force, specific insights into their economic welfare can be derived from the examination of their access to financial resources. Access to monetary resources is an essential element of their quest to achieve the American dream. Indeed, for many African immigrants, the prospect of improving their economic welfare was a critical determinant of their decision to migrate to the United States (Takyi and Konadu-Agyemang 2006). To understand the degree to which Africans are able to achieve this objective, it is necessary to examine whether the contexts in which they work provide differential financial rewards on the basis of their racial and ethnic characteristics.

Race-based inequality in earnings can reflect group differences in other factors known to influence economic success. For example, access to economic resources during the incorporation process varies across time. Accordingly, stylized descriptions of economic incorporation suggest that, partly as a result of their unfamiliarity with the US labor market, immigrants typically have lower earnings than natives in the years immediately following their arrival. With increasing duration of residence, however, their earnings converge with, and in some cases exceed, those of natives (Duleep and Dowhan 2008). Differences in human capital, average working hours, and gender are other factors that could mediate racial differences in earnings (Leicht 2008). Thus, in order to investigate the significance of race and ethnicity in explaining earnings differences among Africans, group differences in these factors also need to be accounted for. If the financial rewards to labor are insensitive to racial and ethnic differences, economic disparities among Africans should disappear after accounting for these additional influences.

Interestingly, several prior studies indicate that these factors fall short of explaining racial and ethnic differences in the earnings of immigrants. Indeed, stylized descriptions of immigrant economic incorporation do not explain why they receive differential financial rewards to labor based on their racial and ethnic differences. Overall, immigrants with racial and/or ethnic minority characteristics typically have lower earnings than Whites (Stewart and Dixon 2010; Reitz and Sklar 1997), while the largest earnings disadvantage is typically found among immigrants with the darkest skin tones (Hersch 2008).

In terms of race, therefore, White Africans are better positioned to receive higher earnings than Black Africans, and this disparity has been confirmed in previous studies. For example, based on their analysis of 1990 census data, Kollehlon and Eule (2003) show that White Africans had higher net hourly earnings than non-White Africans. Still, our understanding of the economic outcomes of Africans remains limited for a number of reasons. For example, similar analyses of racial earnings differences are not available for recent African immigrant groups, while the role of Arab origins in mediating these differences has not been systematically examined. To date, studies on the economic outcomes of African immigrants have also not provided a broader understanding of economic incorporation processes that include an examination of how their racial and ethnic differences influence self-employment outcomes.

Analytically, therefore, the significance of race and Arab ethnicity among African immigrants is the fundamental basis on which economic outcomes such as earnings are examined in this chapter. Increasingly, contemporary African immigrants are also becoming more involved in self-employment activities such as hair braiding, the ownership of ethnic restaurants, and the sale of African products in US flea markets. Discourses on the economic outcomes of Africans should therefore be extended to examine how race influences the participation of African immigrants in self-employment activities. Given the vaunted benefits associated with immigrant self-employment found in several studies, it is also necessary to examine whether the conceptual benefits associated with self-employment help to moderate the racial earnings disparities among African immigrants.

More generally, the chapter examines several explanations for racial differences in the earnings of African immigrants and assesses their validity. It examines whether such differences are rooted in group differences in human-capital endowments. Yet racial economic differences are not just important in themselves; they also have considerable implications for the successful integration of Africans into society. Race-based earnings differences, for example, may be associated with differential exposure to the risks of poverty. A review of the implications of earnings disparities is thus essential for understanding how the consequences of racial and ethnic minority status are likely to affect the economic welfare of African immigrants as they seek to become part of US society.

RACE, ETHNICITY, AND EARNINGS INEQUALITY

The context in which the economic assimilation of Africans occurs is one in which systematic racial and ethnic inequalities have been documented even among the US-born (Oliver and Shapiro 2006). While the wage disadvantage of US-born minorities is partly explained by differences in human capital, there is growing recognition of the fact that it is also a product of discriminatory practices that constrict their earnings capability relative to that of Whites (Darity and Mason 1998).

As with the US-born, immigrants also encounter racially circumscribed opportunities for accumulating wealth. This is particularly true for conventional channels of wealth accumulation such as wages. In general, systematic discrimination, based on race, is likely to result in earnings inequalities among Africans through several critical pathways. First, racial differences can result in differential access to better-paying jobs since being Black is associated with a systematic exclusion from more lucrative job opportunities compared to being White (Huffman and Cohen 2004). Second, even if Black and White Africans are employed in the same occupations, physical differences between both groups may result in different levels of earnings. Here again, the advantage is associated with being White, or more specifically, having features associated with White Europeans. As demonstrated in previous studies, workers with European-looking characteristics generally receive higher wages than workers with darker features (Darity and Mason 1998; Telles and Murguia 1990). A third channel through which racial discrimination can result in economic differences among Africans is related to the influence of discrimination on longer-term income trajectories. In particular, White Africans may have more long-term financial security than Black Africans because being White is further associated with having higher starting wages (Eckstein and Wolpin 1999). In sum, based on physical characteristics alone, non-Arab Whites, who have the most European-looking features among Africans, are more likely to attract higher wages in the US labor market than Black Africans.

Cultural factors such as dress codes, speech patterns, and religious practices are also associated with wage and other types of work-related discrimination (Findley et al. 2005; Grogger 2011). While such ethnic-related disadvantages were highly prevalent following the terrorist attacks of September 11, the net impact of anti-Arab sentiments during this period was more negative for wages than for employment rates and number of working hours (Dávila and Mora 2005; Kaushal, Kaestner, and Reimers 2007). Black Africans are also disadvantaged relative to White Africans, partly as a result of negative media-related influences. Indeed, media stereotypes about Africa have been suggested as a possible negative influence on the earnings of Black African immigrants (Dodoo 1997). Among Africans, ethnic minority status may also trigger perceptions of difference among other members of the US population in ways that have adverse repercussions for earnings. Foreign languages are makers of such differences and could attract discrimination from employers by fueling perceptions of an attachment to a "foreign" culture (Reitz and Sklar 1997). Some of the Black African disadvantage may therefore stem from the fact that Black Africans have lower overall levels of English proficiency than White Africans, and are thus more likely to use foreign languages than their White counterparts.

Ethnic differences among African immigrants therefore have important implications for understanding the dynamics of their economic incorporation processes. In particular, perceptions of cultural differences can result in a wage disadvantage for both Black and Arab-origin Africans relative to non-Arab White Africans. Race, in combination with ethnic differences, can therefore define the boundaries within which Africans acquire resources during the incorporation process. Such boundaries have consistently been observed among immigrants in the post-1965 period. Indeed, considerable variation exists in the economic trajectories of the more racially diverse immigrant groups who arrived after 1965 as compared to White immigrants who arrived before this period. Summing up the contemporary implications of race among immigrants, therefore, Reitz and Sklar (1997) argue that earnings assimilation is distinctively slower among non-White than White immigrants because "race itself (skin color) is penalized, and there is a 'cost of being Black' . . . based on race alone" (235).

Race, Human Capital, and Earnings

Variations in human-capital factors discussed in previous chapters have further implications for racial disparities in earnings among Africans, since greater human capital is associated with higher earnings. Immigrant groups with lower levels of schooling earn less, on average, than those with higher schooling levels. One study of Black immigrants found that Black Africans have higher average schooling than Caribbean Blacks and thus earn higher wages (Dodoo 1997). Significantly, however, higher schooling does not always translate into earnings, even among the Black immigrant population. For example, estimates from the American Community Survey (ACS) indicate that compared to Black immigrants from South America, Black Africans are more likely to be college graduates and about twice as likely to have graduate and professional degrees. Nevertheless, average earnings are about 11 percent lower among Black Africans than among South American Blacks. If schooling is predictive of incomes as expected, White Africans have a logical earnings advantage over Black Africans simply based on their higher comparative schooling levels. Furthermore, if schooling differences are the main factor driving racial earnings disparities among African immigrants, the White advantage should disappear after the net influence of schooling is accounted for.

Beyond differences in schooling, whether one's educational credentials are domestic or foreign also influences earnings just as much as they do the dynamics of occupational attainment. Immigrants with foreign credentials typically experience an earnings penalty compared to US-educated immigrants (Chiswick and Miller 2008). Among Black immigrants, the penalty has been found to be more severe among Black Africans than among Caribbean Blacks (Dodoo 1997). Systematic attempts to examine whether foreign and domestic schooling differences explain racial and ethnic differences in earnings among Africans are lacking. However, their respective influences on occupational status, observed in chapter 4, suggest that the penalty associated with foreign credentials is higher among Black African than among White African immigrants.

Beyond its role as a marker of immigrants' attachment to "foreign" cultures, English proficiency can result in earnings differences through other more direct pathways. On a practical level, English fluency increases immigrant workers' ability to interact with clients, receive instructions from supervisors, and transition from jobs that pay less to those that pay more. Given the significance of these mechanisms, non-Arab White Africans seem better positioned to receive higher wages than Black Africans due to their higher average levels of English proficiency.

The Earnings Profile of African Immigrants

Specific racial and ethnic differences in the earnings of African immigrants are presented in table 5. These estimates use information on annual earnings found in ACS data and refer to annual pretax wage and salary incomes. Overall, the Black-White earnings differentials among Africans are consistent with known patterns of racial inequality among the US-born. In particular, White Africans, regardless of Arab origin, earn considerably more than Black African immigrants. These inequalities are also consistent across gender, and as observed among US natives, the White earnings advantage is particularly driven by the high incomes of White African males. As predicted by cultural frameworks, however, the White African advantage is more distinctive among non-Arab Whites. On average, this group's gross annual earnings are about 135 percent higher than those of the most disadvantaged group, that is, Black Arab Africans. Furthermore, non-Arab Whites earn at least 80 percent more than non-Arab Blacks. This difference, in relative terms, is larger than the comparable Black-White earnings disparity found among the US-born.

TABLE 5. ANNUAL WAGE AND SALARY INCOMES OF AFRICAN IMMIGRANTS

	BLACK ARABS	WHITE ARABS	NON-ARAB BLACKS	NON-ARAB WHITES
All	24,710	40,850	32,290	58,270
Sex				
Male	30,580	52,880	37,390	84,870
Female	15,100	23,240	26,480	30,451
Education				
Less than high school	13,030	13,700	13,320	25,000
High school	16,240	20,860	20,850	29,490
Associate's degree/some college	19,200	28,520	27,220	38,500
College graduates	35,960	52,340	46,660	77,560
Foreign graduates	34,870	43,600	42,940	82,223
US graduates	39,640	68,480	52,544	76,630

DATA SOURCE: 2006–2008 American Community Survey.

Some of the income patterns shown in table 5 are nevertheless inconsistent with the predictions of human-capital theory. For example, racial schooling differences do not appear to explain the overall Black African earnings advantage relative to Whites. Instead, Black Africans earn less than White Africans even after earnings are differentiated by levels of education. Inequalities associated with the interaction between race and Arab ethnicity are also consistent across all levels of schooling. Accordingly, the highest and lowest levels of earnings are found among non-Arab Whites and Black Arab Africans, respectively.

Part of the overall White advantage is driven by the fact that White Africans receive incrementally higher financial rewards to labor than Black Africans as schooling levels increase. For example, among non-Arab Whites, college graduates earn about $57,000 more than individuals who have not completed their high school education. In contrast, among non-Arab Blacks, college graduates can only expect to earn about $30,000 more than their counterparts with less than a high school education. A similar dimension of the unequal racial returns to schooling can be seen by comparing the earnings profiles of White and Black Arab Africans. In particular, although immigrants from both groups earn similar wages among individuals with less than a complete high school education, Black Arabs systematically lag behind their White counterparts as schooling levels increase.

For the most part, African college graduates with US schooling credentials receive higher earnings than their counterparts with foreign credentials. However, the advantage associated with US credentials is more evident in the Arab White African population, among whom US-educated graduates earn about 35 percent more than their counterparts with foreign schooling credentials. The one exception to this trend is found among non-Arab White Africans; in this group, graduates with foreign credentials earn about 7 percent more than their US-educated counterparts. This unique advantage is likely explained by two factors. First, foreign-educated non-Arab Whites are more likely than their US-educated counterparts to have professional credentials beyond their college degrees (such as medical and legal credentials). Such credentials typically attract some of the highest wages in the US labor market. Second, as documented in the previous chapter, foreign-educated non-Arab Whites are typically employed in jobs associated with some of the highest levels of occupational prestige in the US labor market.

Earnings Disparities and Occupations

One major implication of the results discussed above is that Black and White Africans do not appear to receive equal pay for equal schooling. In addition, the data raise important questions regarding the extent to which African immigrants receive equal pay for equal work. Identifying wage disparities for equal work is difficult to demonstrate conclusively without relevant data on the specific demands associated with each job. However, the next best strategy for investigating work-related racial inequalities is to examine whether there are earnings differences between Black and White Africans within occupations or occupational groups.

Figure 10 attempts to do this by examining racial and ethnic differences in earnings among African immigrants within occupational groups, ranked by quintiles of prestige. These quintiles are constructed using occupational SEI indices for all US adults between ages twenty-five and sixty-four. In general, the trends in figure 10 reflect the notion that earnings systematically increase as occupational prestige increases. For example, non-Arab Whites in the least prestigious occupations (first quintile) earn average annual incomes of only about $7,500, while their counterparts in the most prestigious jobs earn about $90,000.

FIGURE 10. EARNINGS DIFFERENCES WITHIN OCCUPATIONAL QUINTILES

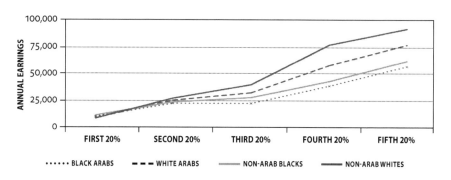

DATA SOURCE: 2006–2008 American Community Survey.

When group differences in earnings are examined, however, considerable racial and ethnic inequalities begin to emerge. Two patterns are important in this regard. First, except within the least prestigious jobs (first quintile), racial and ethnic minority characteristics are consistently associated with an earnings disadvantage within each occupational group. In particular, Black Africans consistently earn less than White Africans in every occupational group beyond the first quintile. Moreover, within each race, Arab-origin Africans earn less than their non-Arab counterparts. A major limitation associated with comparing differences within occupational quintiles, however, is the fact that these quintiles summarize information for more than 300 specific occupations. This limitation can be overcome by additional analysis examining racial earnings differences within each occupation. When further analysis was conducted within specific occupations (i.e., assuming occupations are fixed), the results were consistent with the same patterns of racial and ethnic differences shown in figure 10.

A second pattern captured in these distributions is that racial and ethnic earnings inequalities systematically increase as occupational prestige increases. In practical terms, this tendency implies that the Black African earnings disadvantage is smaller in low-prestige occupations, such as among sanitation workers, but much larger among individuals employed in prestigious jobs such as computer scientists. Surprisingly, figure 10 further indicates that earnings disadvantages associated with race are virtually nonexistent among Africans employed in the least prestigious occupations. In fact, in terms of earnings, White Africans in the first quintile are uncompetitive compared to their Black African counterparts. Specifically, among Africans in the least prestigious occupations White Arabs earn 18 percent less than Black Arab Africans, while non-Arab Whites have about 38 percent lower earnings than their non-Arab Black counterparts.

Assessing Other Social and Demographic Determinants of Earnings Differences

Potentially, a number of factors unrelated to race may explain the earnings disadvantage of Black Africans relative to White Africans. For example, because immigrants with longer US residence have higher earnings than more recent immigrants, higher non-Arab White earnings may simply result from the fact that they have the longest average years of US residence among Africans. Similar differences may explain why White Arabs earn more than both groups of Black Africans since Arab and non-Arab Blacks, on average, have six and three fewer years of US residence respectively than White Arab Africans. Earnings differences may also reflect group differences in weekly working hours. In short, non-Arab Whites may simply earn more than White Arabs because average weekly working hours are longer among the former than among the latter. Differences in US citizenship status, English proficiency, and country of origin are also potential factors that could explain racial earnings inequalities among Africans. To the extent that the data permit, these alternative influences need to be simultaneously accounted for in any attempt to examine the determinants of racial and ethnic earnings inequalities among Africans.

In order to do this, multiple regression analysis is used to determine the extent to which these factors explain overall group differences in earnings. The main outcome of interest in this case is hourly earnings, because variation in annual earnings may reflect differences in hours worked, while hourly earnings are the ideal variable for capturing income differentials in regression analysis (Portes and Zhou 1996). Simplified results from the analysis are presented in figure 11. This figure shows coefficients capturing differences in hourly earnings between four African racial and ethnic minority groups in comparison to non-Arab White Africans (the reference category).

FIGURE 11. DISPARITIES IN HOURLY EARNINGS AMONG AFRICANS IN COMPARISON TO NON-ARAB WHITES

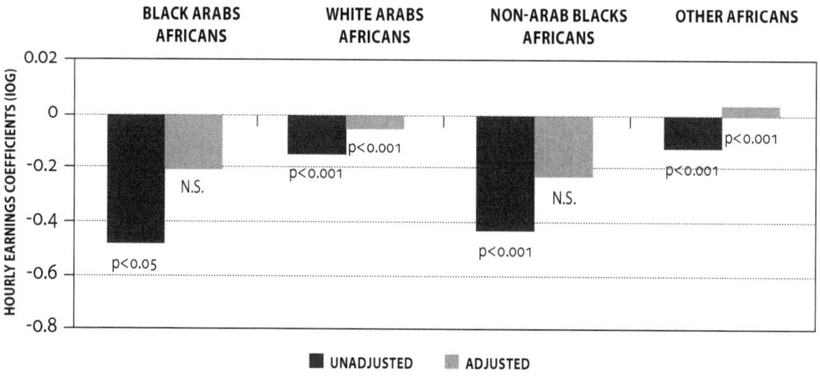

DATA SOURCE: 2006-2008 American Community Survey.
Notes: N.S. means not statistically significant. Dependent variable: log hourly earnings. Adjusted income coefficients are derived from models that control for age, sex, English proficiency, level of schooling, duration of US residence, US citizenship status, and whether or not Africans are from Egypt, Nigeria, and South Africa.

The first set of bars displays unadjusted hourly earnings inequalities between all four groups and non-Arab Whites. In other words, these bars show gross differences in earnings before accounting for the influence of other factors. Among other things, they confirm that the largest comparative earnings disadvantage is found among Black Arab Africans. Likewise, they also show that even the small group of African immigrants who define themselves using other racial markers (e.g., Asian Africans) also has lower gross earnings than non-Arab Whites. The second set of bars depicts adjusted hourly earnings differences in comparison to non-Arab Whites, after accounting for the influence of other factors. They generally show two instructive findings. First, they suggest that the earnings disadvantages of White Arabs and "other" Africans are explained by differences in other factors. As a result, when hourly earnings are adjusted to account for the influence of other social and demographic factors, the relative earnings disadvantage of both groups is entirely eliminated. Second, and more importantly, figure 11 shows that despite adjusting hourly earnings to account for differences in other attributes, the earnings disadvantage of both groups of Black Africans persists.

A number of implications can be derived from these findings. For example, they suggest that lower levels of English proficiency, schooling, and duration of US residence only partly explain the gross earnings disadvantage of Black Africans. After adjusting incomes to account for these influences, the relative Black disadvantage diminishes by about 50 percent among Arab and non-Arab Blacks but is by no means eliminated. Furthermore, the results imply that even if all Africans had similar characteristics, such as age, sex, citizenship status, and language ability, Black Africans would still experience an earnings disadvantage. Black Africans, therefore, experience a wage penalty relative to White Africans over and beyond the disadvantages associated with their lower comparative human-capital characteristics. Consequently, the influence of structural constraints associated with race cannot be discounted as an explanation for the earnings disadvantage of Black Arabs and non-Arab Blacks in the US labor market.

Results from similar analysis of the extent to which other social and demographic factors explain the Black disadvantage among foreign- and US-educated graduates are presented in figure 12. As in the previous figure, each set of bars shows hourly wage differences in comparison to non-Arab Whites (the reference group). In this figure, however, the results focus only on adjusted earnings differences among Africans with foreign and US college credentials. Instructively, they show that even after adjusting for differences in other characteristics, all four groups have lower hourly earnings than non-Arab Whites among foreign-educated Africans. Yet the earnings penalty associated with foreign schooling credentials seems most severe among Black Africans.

FIGURE 12. DISPARITIES IN ADJUSTED HOURLY EARNINGS AMONG AFRICAN COLLEGE GRADUATES IN COMPARISON TO NON-ARAB WHITES

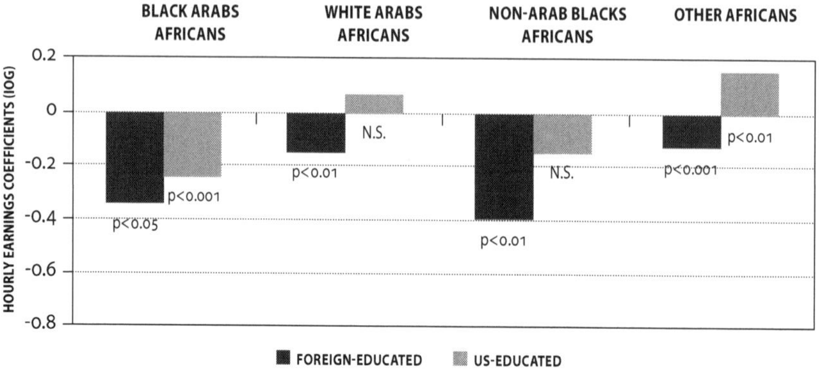

DATA SOURCE: 2006-2008 American Community Survey.
Notes: N.S. means not statistically significant. Dependent variable: log hourly earnings. Adjusted income coefficients are derived from models that control for age, sex, English proficiency, duration of US residence, US citizenship status, and whether or not Africans are from Egypt, Nigeria, and South Africa.

Among US-educated immigrants, however, White Arabs and other Africans, unlike their Black counterparts, do not experience an earnings disadvantage after other differences are accounted for. One interpretation of this finding is that US schooling credentials protect Africans from a relative earnings disadvantage in the labor market only if they are non-Black. Yet, in general, the results imply that regardless of where Black Africans receive their college credentials, or whether they have background characteristics similar to those of White Africans, they experience a unique earnings penalty associated with their racial minority status.

SELF-EMPLOYMENT AND EARNINGS DIFFERENCES

Self-employment provides an additional perspective from which the economic incorporation of African immigrants can be assessed. Although the evidence is inconsistent across groups, self-employment plays a crucial role in the economic mobility of Hispanic, Jewish, and Asian immigrants (Sanders and Nee 1996). Traditionally, the economic success of self-employed immigrants is generally explained by three factors. First, self-employed immigrants are able to draw from a wider pool of labor and financial resources from within their families (Sanders and Nee 1996). Second, self-employed immigrants typically have higher levels of human capital than other immigrants (Maxim 1992); third, they also tend to have higher earnings than other immigrants (Lofstrom 2000). To get a broader perspective on the economic incorporation of African immigrants, therefore, it is important to examine the potential of self-employment activities to serve as a mechanism for ameliorating racial and ethnic earnings inequalities among African immigrants.

To what extent, then, can the conceptual benefits of self-employment ameliorate earnings disparities among Black and White African immigrants? Surprisingly, what we know about self-employment among African immigrants mainly focuses on the outcomes of Black Africans. Many of them, especially those from West African countries such as Senegal, Ghana, and Nigeria, are actively engaged in street trading in various cities in the Northeast. In New York, for example, African street traders are known for selling wares such as masks and statues (Stoller 2002). Opportunities for increasing the earnings of self-employed African immigrants have also increased in recent years as African street traders travel across the United States selling their wares in flea markets (Austin 1994). Currently, a significant number of vendors selling African food products such as smoked fish, snails, and herbs are found in major urban areas in the United States (Chacko 2003; Agbajoh-Laoye 2006). In fact, revenues from self-employment are believed to play an integral role in the economic mobility of recent Black African immigrants. Profits from the hair-braiding businesses of Senegalese immigrants, for example, have allowed low-caste, illiterate braiders to experience considerable levels of social mobility within their communities (Babou 2008).

For several reasons, however, self-employment among Black Africans may not have the same implications for their overall economic welfare as those observed among other immigrants. On average, Africans are still less likely to be self-employed than individuals from other regions such South America and the Middle East, or than US natives (Fairlie and Meyer 1996; Lofstrom 2000). Self-employed Black Africans in particular, also face additional constraints to the economic success of their enterprises. For example, many Black African street traders live in crime-infested neighborhoods and experience precipitous declines in earnings as business slows down during the winter months (Stoller 2001). At the same time, Black Africans who are self-employed are typically not engaged in the types of high-end entrepreneurial activities that produce the economic benefits often observed among other immigrant groups. Apart from hair braiders, whose client base involves US-born Blacks, the clientele of self-employed Blacks is also still very small. Patronage patterns in African grocery stores illustrate this point. In a study conducted by the African-US Chamber of Commerce, African immigrants were found to be more likely to patronize mainstream grocery stores, such as Publix and Safeway, than ethnic food stores (Morse 2009). In fact, the study found that less than one-fifth of all African immigrants actually patronize African grocery stores, and that only 5 percent of Africans patronize specialty stores selling African clothing.

Black Africans may further be excluded from larger, more lucrative types of business ventures as a result of systematic patterns of race-based institutional discrimination. For example, lending discrimination by US financial institutions has traditionally had a negative effect on the likelihood that Blacks will enter productive self-employment ventures (Fairlie 1999). Indeed, among US Blacks, street trading is considered to be a direct consequence of their economic marginalization by mainstream US institutions (Austin 1994).

Contextual influences also limit the extent to which the typical economic advantages associated with self-employment are found among Black Africans. Many self-employed Black Africans have linguistic or educational disadvantages that limit their options for employment in the formal sector. For example, African street traders and hair braiders generally have low levels of English proficiency that serve as a constraint to productivity. One study indicates that the apparent unwillingness of African braiders to learn English is a significant source of tension between them and their clients (Babou 2008). The legal contexts in which various self-employed Black Africans operate impose further constraints to the profitability of their operations. Estimates indicate, for example, that about 90 percent of all merchant arrests in New York involve Senegalese Murid immigrants who are predominantly street traders (Babou 2002). African street traders also include a significant number of undocumented immigrants (Austin 1994). In addition, self-employed Black Africans are sometimes victims of hate crimes associated with their racial and ethnic minority status (Dolnick 2009).

In general, these contextual influences suggest that for Black Africans, self-employment is a constraint and not a facilitator of wealth accumulation. As a result, the significance of self-employment seems to revolve around its role as a means of sustenance among Black Africans, because of the structural disadvantages they encounter associated with their race. In contrast to other immigrants, therefore, Black Africans who are self-employed are not driven by the attraction to high income rewards but by the need for survival. More generally, if hostile contexts are differentially encountered across race and ethnicity, they will likely result in economic inequalities that negatively affect the well-being of African immigrants with racial and ethnic minority characteristics.

PATTERNS OF SELF-EMPLOYMENT AND EARNINGS AMONG AFRICAN IMMIGRANTS

Contemporary African immigrants are not very different from the overall immigrant population of the United States in terms of their likelihood of being self-employed. Both groups have about 10 percent of their populations between ages twenty-five and sixty-four involved in self-employment activities. Africans also share similarities with the US-born in terms of racial differences in self-employment. Like US-born Blacks, for example, Black Africans seem to encounter more constraints on entry into self-employment than their White counterparts. Thus, in table 6, the estimates indicate that non-Arab Black Africans are about half as likely to be self-employed as non-Arab Whites. The background characteristics of self-employed Africans further indicate that self-employed Black Africans considerably differ from self-employed Whites in terms of levels of schooling. Among White Africans, for example, the majority of the self-employed are college graduates. However, the opposite is true among Black Arabs and non-Arab Blacks.

TABLE 6. PERCENTAGE OF WORKERS WHO ARE SELF-EMPLOYED AND SELF-EMPLOYMENT EARNINGS AMONG AFRICAN IMMIGRANTS

	BLACK ARABS	WHITE ARABS	NON-ARAB BLACKS	NON-ARAB WHITES
Percent self-employed	8.7	14.0	8.2	16.5
Annual self-employment earnings				
All	21,710	37,340	21,565	47,608
Male	24,410	40,270	23,064	64,900
Female	5,540	26,112	17,360	15,970

DATA SOURCE: 2006–2008 American Community Survey.

Foreign-educated African college graduates are also more likely to be self-employed than African immigrants with similar US credentials. These differences are consistent with the notion that self-employment serves as an alternative income-generating activity among African immigrants who face difficulties securing employment in the formal sector of the economy. If this notion is correct, the results would suggest that such constraints are more relevant for understanding the outcomes of self-employed Black Arabs. Disadvantaged on the basis of their race, ethnicity, and place of schooling, foreign-educated Black Arabs have the highest rates of self-employment of the four African race-ethnic groups.

When annual earnings are examined, however, it becomes clear that the average earnings of self-employed Africans are well below the corresponding group averages reported in table 5. Furthermore, in line with the disadvantage associated with racial minority characteristics, Black Africans continue to have lower annual earnings than White Africans even among the self-employed. One interpretation of this is that race-based structural constraints still have negative implications for earnings, even in the absence of employer prejudices that could affect earnings. Racial differences in annual earnings are, however, driven by gender-related earnings disparities. Black Arabs, for example, would clearly earn higher average incomes than non-Arab Blacks if female earnings in both groups were the same. Likewise, the overall non-Arab White advantage seems directly related to the fact that non-Arab White males earn considerably more than other African immigrants. In terms of Arab-ethnicity, there is a clear earnings disadvantage of White-Arabs relative to non-Arab White Africans. A similar disparity is not seen among Black Africans. This may result from the fact that self-employed Black Arabs are more educated than their non-Arab Black counterparts. For that reason, they may be more able to navigate ethnic-related constrains to the profitability of self-employment ventures faced by members of their race.

As done in the examination of overall earnings differences, further inves-tigation, using regression analysis, is required to assess the extent to which disparities in self-employment earnings are explained by other factors. Results from the regression analysis of the hourly earnings of self-employed Africans are therefore presented in figure 13. When adjusted and unadjusted earnings differences are compared, it is clear that even after accounting for differences in other characteristics, the usual pattern of racial inequality among Africans per-sists. Accordingly, the earnings disadvantage among the self-employed is greater among Black than non-Black Africans. Lower earnings among self-employed non-Arab Blacks in particular are explained neither by differences in conven-tional determinants of earnings, such as human-capital endowments, nor by factors such as duration of US residence or citizenship status.

All together, these findings suggest that Black African immigrants face sig-nificant structural disadvantages associated with their race even when involved in self-employment activities. Consequently, these disadvantages would limit the earnings Black Africans derive from self-employment prospects even if they had social and demographic characteristics similar to those of White Africans.

The vaunted advantages associated with immigrant self-employment are thus unlikely to diminish the overall economic disadvantage of Black African immigrants relative to White Africans. Clearly, the constraints associated with racial minority status are still important for understanding the economic well-being of Africans, even when economic incorporation is conceived of in terms of the opportunities available in self-employment activities.

FIGURE 13. DISPARITIES IN HOURLY EARNINGS AMONG SELF-EMPLOYED AFRICANS IN COMPARISON TO NON-ARAB WHITES

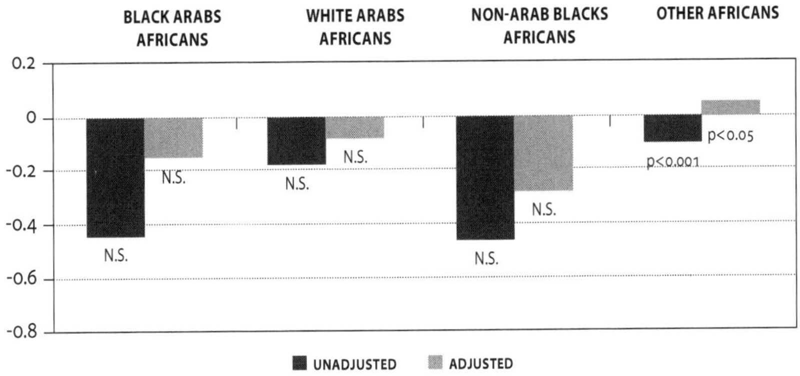

Notes: N.S. means not statistically significant at the $p < 0.5$ level. Dependent variable: log hourly earnings. Adjusted income coefficients are derived from models that control for age, sex, English proficiency, level of schooling, duration of US residence, US citizenship status, and whether or not Africans are from Egypt, Nigeria, and South Africa.

SUMMARY AND IMPLICATIONS

Earnings differences, conditional on race and ethnicity, are direct indicators of economic inequality among African immigrants, and, as expected, these immigrants experience significant earnings differences conditional on their race and ethnicity. The evidence suggests that racial earnings inequalities also exist among Africans employed in similar types of jobs. In terms of self-employment, there are a number of reasons explaining why African-owned businesses, especially those owned by Black Africans, do not experience the vaunted earnings benefits associated with immigrant self-employment. African hair braiders, for example, face linguistic constraints that negatively affect their relationships with their clients. Other constraints are structural; for example, Black Africans are likely to be exposed to the same patterns of race-based lending discrimination known to constrict the economic prospects of Black-owned businesses. Racial and ethnic comparisons of the prevalence of self-employment as well as self-employment earnings thus underscore the main dimensions of self-employment inequality among Africans in the labor market.

All things considered, earnings differences have far-reaching implications for the welfare of African immigrants as they integrate into society. The most obvious of them is that the racial dimensions of these differences will facilitate the assimilation of African immigrants into already established patterns of economic inequality in the US population. For Black Africans in particular, the earnings disadvantage will further restrict prospects for their economic mobility in subsequent generations, since the earnings penalty associated with racial minority status is likely to persist across time.

In the long run, these economic differences may simply reproduce the same patterns of inequality across immigrant generations. In each of these generations, therefore, Black Africans are likely to lack the degree of financial stability enjoyed by their White African counterparts. One consequence of this is that the children of Black immigrants are likely to receive more limited income transfers from previous generations than their counterparts with White African parents. Although these have not yet been documented among Black Africans, evidence from Black Caribbean immigrants indicates that the children of middle-class parents have considerably higher socioeconomic status than children of parents with a lower comparative status (Waters 1999). Racially constricted earnings patterns will thus ensure that in subsequent generations the descendants of Black Africans will lag behind those of their White counterparts in terms of level of savings, ownership of assets, and the capacity to create wealth.

A more immediate implication of the earnings inequality among Africans relates to its association with patterns of exposure to poverty. Estimates from the US census show racial and ethnic poverty disparities similar to those observed in earnings. Specifically, poverty rates among Africans are considerably higher among Arab Blacks (28 percent) and non-Arab Blacks (19.4 percent) than among White Arabs (13 percent) and non-Arab Whites (8.1 percent). Racial minority status also makes it difficult for Black immigrants to use their human-capital endowments to escape the grip of poverty. In fact, Black Africans have higher child poverty rates than Asian and White immigrants, despite the fact that Black African household heads have higher levels of schooling than their White and Asian counterparts (Thomas 2011b). Part of this overall Black African poverty disadvantage stems from the fact that poverty declines less rapidly among Black than non-Black immigrants as parental human capital increases.

At the same time, the economic consequences of racial minority status are particularly serious among Black African refugee immigrants. Comparisons between Black immigrant refugees, many of whom come from Africa, and their non-Black counterparts indicate that the former have higher rates of child poverty than the latter (Thomas 2011b). Furthermore, in Minnesota, a major resettlement destination for African refugees, the average earnings of Africans were 50 percent lower than those of White natives in 2006, while half of Africans in the state lived in poverty (A. Hughes 2006).

Differences in economic resources may also have further repercussions for disparities in the residential characteristics and spatial assimilation of African immigrants. Since earnings are positively associated with neighborhood characteristics, for example, high incomes among non-Arab Whites makes them better positioned than Black Africans to move into neighborhoods with better educational, recreational, and other types of social infrastructure. The specific residential characteristics of Black and White Africans have, however, not been examined in existing studies. Nevertheless, available evidence suggests that many Black African immigrants live in unfavorable neighborhood contexts, as a result of both low incomes and systematic disadvantages associated with their race. For very poor Black African immigrants, this results in living in low-cost housing communities and experiencing significant obstacles in securing alternative types of housing in high-quality neighborhoods (Hollish 2010).

All together, the economic dimensions of African immigrant incorporation, yet again, underscore the significance of race in their efforts to integrate into US society. These dimensions are, however, less important for understanding how race and Arab ethnicity influence their integration into the social fabric of the United States. Social integration processes are better understood by examining the dynamics of interpersonal relationships between African immigrants and US-natives. Assessing the racial dimensions of these relationships and their social implications will provide additional insights into the processes through which Black and White African immigrants become incorporated into the social mainstream.

Race, Ethnicity, and Marital Incorporation

C ultural differences that affect interpersonal relationships are among the most significant barriers that immigrants encounter during the incorporation process. Unlike differences in outcomes such as occupational status and incomes, cultural differences between immigrants and natives also tend to persist for much longer. One consequence of this is that immigrants can experience increasing economic mobility but still lag behind in terms of their degree of integration into the social mainstream. Complete social integration is facilitated by the formation of viable interpersonal relationships between immigrants and natives. Few indicators capture the dynamics of such relationships as well as those related to intermarriage. As a result, the likelihood of intermarriage between immigrants and natives is considered to be a critical measure of immigrants' structural assimilation and integration. The analysis of such marriages is also usually used to assess Gordon's (1964) proposition that immigrants' integration into the structure of society is the final stage of the assimilation process. Accordingly, the most assimilated groups are expected to have the highest rates of intermarriage since such marriages reflect the fact that cultural boundaries no longer act as constraints on intergroup relations.

Ethnic and racial differences are nevertheless among the major determinants of intermarriage (Lucassen and Laarman 2009; van Tubergen and Maas 2007), and this is exemplified by the wide disparity in intermarriage rates among racial and ethnic groups (Jacobs and Labov 2002; Bean et al. 2005). Latinos and

Asians, for example, have higher intermarriage rates than Blacks (Qian and Lichter 2007); however, both groups have lower intermarriage rates than Native Americans (Kalmijn 1998). These variations are generally a product of a number of influences, including, among other things, differences in the perceived attractiveness of potential spouses, based on their racial and ethnic characteristics (Lee and Edmonston 2005; Yancey 2009). Additionally, because social and economic attributes affect the formation of such marriages, it is also possible for racial and ethnic intermarriage differences to be undergirded by socioeconomic factors (Merton 1941; Fu 2001).

Racial diversity among African immigrants therefore has several implications for their expected patterns of marital incorporation. The most obvious is that racial differences in marital incorporation among immigrants have been found to be consistent with the racial intermarriage patterns of the US-born (Sassler 2005; Qian and Lichter 2001). Furthermore, ethnic differences, especially between Arab and non-Arabs, are likely to create additional disparities in the speed with which cultural differences between Africans and US natives decline. Specifically, intermarriage differences can reflect variations in the social distance between US natives and specific immigrant groups (Pagnini and Morgan 1990; Rosenfeld 2002). Accordingly, Arab and non-Arab intermarriage differences can therefore be used to evaluate the extent to which cultural stereotypes of Arabs impede or facilitate interpersonal relations with US natives. If they impede interactions in the form of romantic relationships, for example, non-Arab Africans should be more likely to intermarry with US natives than Arab Africans.

Differential intermarriage rates further have economic implications because they directly affect the economic welfare of immigrant families. According to Meng and Gregory (2005) intermarriage between immigrants and the US-born is positively related to family incomes. Significantly, their analysis indicates that this income premium is not observed among immigrants in endogamous marriages, that is, among immigrants who marry within their own group. As much as race and ethnicity are important for understanding marital outcomes, however, surprisingly little is known about the marital patterns of African immigrant groups or the determinants of their likelihood of intermarriage.

In considering the marital incorporation processes of African immigrants, therefore, a number of issues need to be addressed. As a backdrop for the investigation of racial and ethnic differences, we first need to develop a general sense of the social dynamics of marriage in African immigrant communities. This can be achieved by reviewing the evidence from existing studies on marriage and family relationships among African immigrants. Next, the possible mechanisms contributing to racial differences in intermarriage between Africans and the US-born need to be articulated. For example, how is the racial hierarchy of spousal preferences of US natives likely to affect the intermarriage prospects of Black and White Africans? Are group differences in educational attainment also likely to explain intermarriage disparities among African immigrants? Finally, specific differences in the intermarriage rates of African immigrant groups need to be examined using empirical evidence. Accordingly, data from the ACS are used to describe and explain racial and ethnic variations in intermarriage among African immigrants. This three-pronged strategy is then used to draw conclusions concerning differential patterns of structural assimilation among African immigrant groups and their relevance for understanding racial color lines.

The Social Dynamics of Marriage among African Immigrants

There is limited research on the dynamics of marriage in African immigrant communities. However, existing studies provide useful insights into the significance of marriage and its role in shaping the incorporation processes of African immigrants. Married African couples, for example, typically migrate to the United States in sequential patterns characterized by the initial migration of husbands followed by their wives (Kamya 2005). Actual marital decisions among single African immigrants, however, involve the choice of selecting spouses in the United States or in African origin countries. Much of what we know about this process relates to the decisions of single, male immigrants. In particular, single males who choose to marry spouses in Africa either return home to select a spouse or have one selected for them by family members (Arthur 2000). Nevertheless, as mentioned earlier, research on marital incorporation suggests that individuals in marriages involving couples from similar ethnic origins are less assimilated than those in marriages between immigrants and natives. Immigrant couples in African-only marriages thus tend to have families that incorporate many of the cultural norms found in African societies. For example, couples in such marriages tend to practice traditional gender roles, have limited public displays of affection, and largely participate in traditional rites such as naming ceremonies (Kamya 2005; McAdoo, Younge, and Getahun 2007). Likewise, married couples from Africa consider themselves to be part of a larger configuration of extended family units (Kamya 2005). As a result, extended family members in Africa are sometimes consulted in the process of resolving marital problems and other challenges faced by African families in the United States (Orieny 2008).

Endogenous marriages, with only African spouses, therefore operate in ways that differ from the dynamics of marriages in Western societies. Yet research indicates that among married African couples, a longer period of US residence results in a lower likelihood of maintaining traditional cultural values (McAdoo, Younge, and Getahun 2007). Declining adherence to these values may also be accompanied by the acquisition of new perceptions concerning marriage that are more consistent with those held by US natives. With increasing US residence, therefore, the ways in which marriages are negotiated among African couples changes. One example of this is that economic pressures within immigrant families have been known to increase the significance of wives as income earners, in ways that challenge traditional African norms concerning gender roles and relationships between spouses (Kamya 2005).

Variations in the adherence to patriarchal traditions in African immigrant communities also influence the dynamics of marriage and the prospects of intermarriage with US natives. Vaughn and Holloway (2010), for example, found strong patterns of patriarchy among African Muslim immigrants, unlike those reported in other studies. Similar patterns of patriarchy also exist among Arab immigrants, broadly defined (Kulczycki and Lobo 2002). In general, however, patriarchal traditions influence the dynamics of intermarriage by constraining the marital choices of immigrants in ways that undermine their intermarriage prospects with US natives. Arab patriarchal traditions, for example, are a major constraint on the formation of marital unions between Arab immigrants and non-Arabs (Abu-Laban and Abu-Laban 1999; Kulczycki and Lobo 2002). Interestingly, these constraints are more important for understanding the marital outcomes of the daughters than those of the sons of Arab immigrants.

Given the social dynamics of marriage among African immigrants, it seems clear that Africans who choose to marry US-born spouses will be involved in fundamental shifts in the social context of marriage. These shifts will be accompanied by a declining attachment to traditional African norms governing issues such as spousal selection. Furthermore, as cultural boundaries between Africans and US natives disappear, intermarriage will involve the acquisition of new perceptions of marriage that result from the process of negotiating new expectations concerning marriage. Marital incorporation will also involve the process of de-emphasizing the influence of patriarchal traditions in ways that increase interpersonal relations between Arab Africans, for example, and the US-born. At the same time, shifts in social and cultural dynamics are not the only processes likely to affect the formation of intimate relationships between Africans and US natives. Beyond these influences in particular is the role of racial color lines in providing the parameters around which such relationships are formed.

Intermarriage and the Racial Color Line

The social context in which intermarriage between Africans and US natives occurs is one in which a distinct color line separates Black and White marriages, despite progress in racial integration in other US institutions (Batson, Qian, and Lichter 2006). Although interracial marriages have increased since the 1970s, such marriages still account for a small proportion of all US marriages since Blacks and Whites still overwhelmingly marry spouses within their own race (Fu and Heaton 2008; Waters and Eschbach 1995). Among the limited number of US interracial marriages, there is also a distinct pattern of spousal racial characteristics that underlie the continued significance of contemporary color lines. In particular, interracial marriages among non-White groups are more likely to involve marriages to White rather than Black spouses (Lee and Edmonston 2005). In other words, non-White individuals choosing to marry spouses of another race tend to select spouses from the very top rather than the bottom of the US racial hierarchy.

These general trends are important for understanding how racial color lines will influence the marital incorporation of African immigrants for two reasons. First, because of the continued significance of same-race marriages, Africans who marry US-born spouses are likely to marry spouses with whom they share similar racial characteristics. Second, as a result of the greater tendency of White spouses to be selected in interracial marriages compared to other spouses, Black and White African immigrants are likely to have disparate prospects of forming interracial unions with US natives as they become more socially integrated.

These expectations are supported by studies on interracial marriages among the Black population of the United States. Batson, Qian, and Lichter (2006), for example, observe that Black African immigrants are generally more likely to have US-born Black than US-born White spouses. However, their analysis does not distinguish between the outcomes of Arab and non-Arab Black Africans. In terms of marriage across race, they also observe that Black immigrants are less likely than US-born Blacks to have White spouses. Yet another observation reported in their study is the fact that opportunities for interracial marriage with US natives vary across gender. When interracial marriages occurred among Black immigrants, they were more likely to involve a Black male marrying a

White female than a Black female and a White male.

Bean and Stevens (2003) further observe distinct racial patterns in their more general investigation of the marital outcomes of Black and White immigrants. According to their study, Black immigrants are less likely to marry White spouses compared to immigrants who are White, Asian, or Hispanic. Furthermore, their analysis suggests that White immigrants who intermarry with US natives typically marry spouses who are non-Black rather than Black. In addition, they report that spousal combinations involving White immigrants and US-born Black spouses are less prevalent than those consisting of Black immigrants and US-born White spouses. A major possibility raised by these findings, therefore, is the likelihood that Black and White immigrants make different racial choices when deciding to marry US-born spouses.

Perceptions concerning the desirability of specific racial attributes are among the key mechanisms likely to influence the intermarriage prospects of African immigrants. Two perspectives are important in this regard. The first is found in a growing number of studies supporting the view that a racial status hierarchy is used to determine the desirability of potential mates. As expected, White potential spouses are generally preferred to potential spouses from racial minority groups (Fu 2001; Heaton and Jacobson 2000). Instructively, however, similar patterns of skin tone desirability have also been observed in the spousal selection processes of selected racial minority groups. In some contexts, for example, Black males have been found to consider lighter-skinned women more attractive than darker-looking women (Kulczycki and Lobo 2002). This first perspective therefore suggests that because of the premium placed on Whiteness in romantic relationships, US natives will consider White Africans to be more preferable spouses than Black African immigrants.

A more nuanced perspective on spousal preferences is, however, provided by Durodoye and Coker (2008), who argue that Black African immigrants who marry US natives tend to prefer spouses who are Black rather than White. According to this perspective, cultural similarities between Black Africans and US-born Blacks underlie the shared attraction between both groups. For example, Black Africans and US-born Blacks share a strong communal orientation connecting nuclear and extended families, while also sharing a deep sense of spirituality. Notably, Durodoye and Coker (2008) indicate that Black Africans and US-born Blacks also share cultural traditions emphasizing a high degree of resiliency in the face of challenges. These traditions could provide a stronger connection between Black Africans and Black Africans than the connections found between the former and US-born Whites.

OTHER DETERMINANTS OF INTERMARRIAGE DIFFERENCES

Religious differences are also possible determinants affecting intermarriage between Africans and the US-born, although their influence is generally similar to that found in patriarchal communities. Differences in the major religions practiced by Arab-Africans, the majority of whom are Muslims, and US natives are expected to be particularly more defined. As observed by Kaufman (2008), intermarriage rates between Muslims and natives are particularly low in the predominantly Christian societies of the West. Nevertheless, there is very little empirical research on intermarriage between Arab immigrants and US natives. One study by Kulczycki and Lobo (2002) indicates that intermarriage between Arab immigrants and the US-born is much higher among Arabs from largely Christian backgrounds, mainly those in non-African countries, than among predominantly Muslim Arab immigrants. Low rates of intermarriage between Muslim immigrants and natives partly reflect significant social pressures against interfaith marriages among Islamic immigrant communities (Abu-Laban and Abu-Laban 1999). Since African Arabs come from predominantly Islamic backgrounds, their rates of intermarriage with members of the US-born population are likely to be very low. If such marriages occur, however, they are more likely to involve marriages between US natives with White Arab rather than Black Arab spouses. This is because, unlike Black Arabs, White Arabs have the racial characteristics presumed to be preferred in romantic relationships by US natives, and are more likely to have socioeconomic characteristics (such as higher earnings) attractive to potential spouses.

Differences in acculturation measures such as English proficiency and years of US residence will also influence the dynamics of intermarriage between Africans and the US-born. Immigrants who speak English proficiently tend to marry US-born spouses at higher rates than their nonproficient counterparts, because English facilitates social interactions that decrease social distances relative to the US-born (Pagnini and Morgan 1990). Longer years of US residence and, by implication, greater acculturation also increase the likelihood that immigrants will intermarry with natives for some of the reasons noted earlier. African immigrant groups with more average years of US residence (e.g., White Africans) are thus expected to have greater prospects of intermarriage than immigrants in more recently arrived subgroups.

Education, gender, and group-size differences generally contribute to intermarriage differences in the following specific ways. First, individuals with more education typically marry across race and ethnicity more than their less educated counterparts (Batson, Qian, and Lichter 2006; Kulczycki and Lobo 2002). Presumably, education facilitates the use of objective criteria other than nativity or racial attributes in drawing important conclusions. Second, in terms of gender, males are more likely to marry out of their subgroup than females (Jacobs and Labov 2002). Third, groups with smaller sizes generally have more exogamous marriages, that is, marry out of their own subgroup, than groups with larger populations (Blau, Blum, and Schwartz 1982; Kalmijn 1993). In general, this suggests that despite their smaller size relative to other African immigrant groups, Black Arab Africans have an overall advantage in terms of their possibilities of intermarriage.

RACIAL PATTERNS OF MARITAL UNION AMONG AFRICANS

To begin the empirical analysis of the marital incorporation of African immigrants, we briefly review their overall marriage patterns, because intermarriages are only a subset of all African immigrant marriages. Information on group differences in marriage rates also provides important insights concerning the overall prevalence of marriage across racial and ethnic groups. Previous empirical research on the prevalence of marriage among African immigrants is mainly restricted to comparisons showing that Black Africans have higher marriage rates than US-born Blacks and other Black immigrants (Kent 2007). Although this insight is informative, it does not provide clarity on the question of whether there are racial differences in the prevalence of marriage among African immigrant subgroups.

Racial and ethnic marriage estimates for adults age eighteen and above are therefore presented in figure 14. Among Blacks, they confirm that marriage is more prevalent among Black Africans, regardless of Arab ethnicity, than among US-born Blacks. This comparatively higher marriage rate is driven by the outcomes of non-Arab Blacks from Guinea, Nigeria, and Eritrea as well as the marriage patterns of Black Arab immigrants from Egypt and Morocco. More importantly, there are distinct racial and gender patterns in the prevalence of marriage shown in the figure. For example, among racial and ethnic groups, marital unions are most prevalent among White Africans, especially White Arab immigrants, among whom close to three-quarters of all adults are married. The highest marriage rates in the data are specifically found among White Arabs from Egypt, Morocco, and Sudan. Figure 14, however, shows that although non-Arab Whites have slightly lower marriage rates than White Arabs, they are still more likely to be married than individuals in both Black immigrant groups. Marriage is, further, more prevalent among White Africans than among US-born Whites and US-born Blacks. On average, Blacks have lower marriage rates than Whites among both immigrants and natives. Furthermore, in terms of gender, comparatively larger gender gaps associated with comparatively lower female marriage rates are observed among both Black African groups and US-born Blacks. Two possibilities are likely to account for this. They include the higher levels of remarriage among males than females and the relatively limited number of economically attractive Black males available as potential husbands to Black females (Lichter, LeClere, and McLaughlin 1991; Smith, Zick, and Duncan 1991).

Race, Ethnicity, and the Prevalence of Intermarriage among African Immigrants

Turning our attention to intermarriage patterns, table 7 shows that regardless of race, African immigrants are less likely to have US-born than non-US-born spouses. In fact, in three of the four major race-ethnic groups, less than a third of all adult immigrants are actually married to US-born spouses. Racial and ethnic patterns of intermarriage are, however, similar to the broader marriage patterns shown in figure 14. For example, intermarriage levels are higher among White than Black Africans among both Arab and non-Arabs. A major implication of these differences is that they support the notion that White Africans have

FIGURE 14. PERCENTAGE MARRIED AMONG IMMIGRANTS AND THE US-BORN

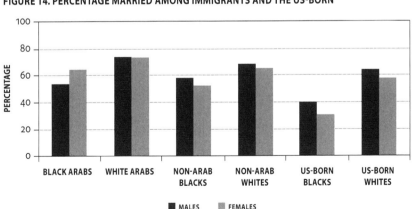

DATA SOURCE: 2006–2008 American Community Survey.

greater prospects for developing intimate relationships with the US-born than Black Africans. Furthermore, the estimates suggest that these prospects are even greater for non-Arab Whites than for their Arab counterparts. In particular, unlike any other African immigrant group, half of all non-Arab Whites are married to US-born spouses.

In terms of duration of residence, table 7 shows that, on average, Africans with the longest years of US residence have a higher tendency of intermarrying with US natives than recently arrived Africans. Perceived cultural differences between Africans and the US-born therefore tend to decline as Africans become more acculturated. Moreover, longer years of US residence also facilitate more long-term interactions between both groups. A major exception to this tendency is found among White Arabs. As shown in the table, White Arabs with less than ten years of US residence have, surprisingly, the highest rates of intermarriage within their group. More detailed analysis of the data reveals interesting differences in the racial composition of the US-born spouses of recent White Arab immigrants compared to those of their longer-term counterparts. In particular, White Arabs with less than ten years of US residence are more likely

TABLE 7. THE DISTRIBUTION OF AFRICAN IMMIGRANT MARRIAGES TO US-BORN SPOUSES

	BLACK ARABS	WHITE ARABS	NON-ARAB BLACKS	NON-ARAB WHITES
Percentage married to US-born spouses				
All	11.8	27.7	17.8	50
Males	13.5	29.6	21.3	49.6
Female	9.7	13.0	11.4	50.4
By duration of residence cohort				
0 to 9 years	12.3	24.8	15.2	40.3
10 to 19 years	6.2	5.7	14.9	34.1
20 to 29 years	3.1	8.1	18.7	46.5
30-plus years	30	9.6	28.1	68.8
By educational attainment				
Less than high school	2.6	19.5	10.3	37.4
High school	12.5	35.4	17.4	50.3
Associate's degree	15.4	36.4	15.6	59.2
College graduate	13.5	24.7	18.1	50.1

DATA SOURCE: 2006–2008 American Community Survey: Adults age 18 and above.

to marry US-born spouses who were non-White (62 percent) than those with at least thirty years of US residence (32 percent). Marital incorporation thus occurs more rapidly among recent than among long-term White-Arabs because they are seem comparatively less influenced by the perceived desirability of Whiteness in spousal selection decisions.

No systematic relationship is shown between intermarriage and educational attainment, in contrast to research suggesting that more schooling positively influences the likelihood of intermarriage. Among White Arabs, for example, immigrants with a high-school education are more likely to marry US natives than those who are college graduates, while the reverse is true among non-Arab Blacks. One of the consistent relationships shown between intermarriage and schooling, however, is that across all groups, immigrants with less than a high-school education are generally less likely to intermarry than those with college degrees. Table 7 also shows that except among non-Arab Blacks, the highest levels of intermarriage are found among immigrants with an associate's degree. Accordingly, for most African immigrants additional schooling beyond an associate's degree does not result in an increase in the prospects of marrying a US-born spouse.

Accounting for Racial and Ethnic Intermarriage Differences

A more systematic attempt is made to explain racial and ethnic intermarriage differences using odds ratios from logistic regression analyses. These analyses are done separately for males and females, and the results are presented in figures 15 and 16 respectively. These analyses attempt to answer two questions. First, what happens to racial and ethnic intermarriage differences after accounting for group differences in factors such as educational attainment, duration of residence, and English-language proficiency? Second, do group differences in these characteristics explain racial and ethnic intermarriage differences in similar ways among African males and females?

Two sets of estimates showing the odds of intermarriage among African immigrant males are presented in figure 15. Non-Arab Whites are used as the comparison group; as a result, 1.00 on the vertical axis represents the point of no difference with non-Arab Whites. The first set of bars presents the estimated odds of intermarriage, which adjust only for differences in age. As the estimates indicate, racial differences in intermarriage persist even after accounting for age differences. Despite adjusting for age differences, for example, the odds of

FIGURE 15. ADJUSTED ODDS OF MALE INTERMARRIAGE COMPARED TO NON-ARAB WHITES

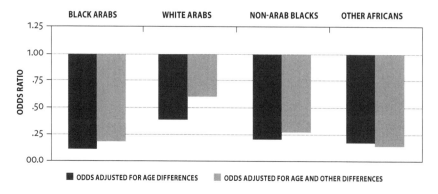

FIGURE 16. ADJUSTED ODDS OF FEMALE INTERMARRIAGE COMPARED TO NON-ARAB WHITES

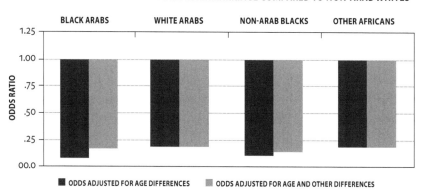

DATA SOURCE: 2006–2008 American Community Survey.
Notes: All estimates are statistically significant at the p<0.5 level. Dependent variable is whether or not African immigrants are married to US-born spouses. Adjusted odds for age and other differences also include controls for, sex, English proficiency, level of schooling, duration of US residence, and country of origin dummy variables.

intermarriage are still comparatively lower among Black African males, especially among Black Arab males, than among White Africans. Similarly, African males in the residual category of other Africans (including non-Black and non-White Africans) also marry US-born spouses at lower rates than non-Arab Whites.

When differences in age and other factors, including English proficiency and education, are accounted for in the second set of bars in figure 15, notable decreases are observed in the relative disadvantage of intermarriage among Blacks, in general, and among the two Arab groups, especially among White Arabs. These reductions are consistent with the notion that Arab Africans have low levels of English proficiency that may negatively affect social interactions with US natives. Instructively, the second set of bars suggests that had there been no group differences in factors such as education, duration of residence, and English-language proficiency, White Arab males, in particular, would have had slightly higher intermarriage rates than the rates actually observed. The second set of estimates also shows that non-White African males, including Black Africans, fare less well in terms of intermarriage with the US-born than non-Arab Whites, even after accounting for group differences in other factors. Thus, although the generally high levels of schooling and incomes of White Africans make them attractive in the US marriage market, these differences do not explain their high prospects of intermarriage relative to those of Black Africans.

Estimates for females shown in figure 16 tell a similar story concerning intermarriage differences between non-Arab White and other African females. Accordingly, after adjusting for age differences, females in each of the four groups continue to have lower odds of intermarriage than their non-Arab White counterparts. Unlike males (figure 15), however, there is no evidence showing that in comparative terms, White Arab females have better prospects of marrying US-born spouses than Black African females, nor are there large intermarriage differences between Arabs and non-Arabs. Among Black, Arab White, and other African females, however, the comparative odds of intermarriage relative to non-Arab Whites in the second set of bars remain virtually similar to those in the first despite the additional adjustments made for other factors. Consequently, we can conclude that differences in factors such as education, English proficiency, and duration of residence play practically no role in explaining the lower intermarriage rates among African females with racial and ethnic minority characteristics. In fact, figure 15 suggests that non-Arab White females have better prospects of marrying US natives than other females, among African immigrants similarly acculturated in terms of English proficiency and years of US residence.

Additional insights into the determinants of intermarriage across gender are provided by more comprehensive analysis of the data not reported in these figures. They show, for example, that educational attainment and country-of-origin differences do not have similar associations with intermarriage among African males and females. In terms of education, for example, immigrants who are high-school and college graduates are most likely to have US-born spouses among females but not among males. Females from selected origin countries such as Morocco and Kenya also have higher odds of intermarriage than other African females. Yet, in comparison, there is no evidence showing that males from these countries have higher odds of intermarriage than other African males.

Spousal Racial Characteristics of African Immigrants Who Intermarry

Also relevant for understanding marital incorporation processes is the question of whether group differences exist in the racial characteristics of the US-born spouses of African immigrants. To address this question, the racial characteristics of the spouses of African males and females who intermarry with the US-born are presented in figures 17 and 18. As expected, marital incorporation among African immigrants involves a high degree of racial endogamy. Regardless of sex, White Africans are more likely to marry White than Black US-born spouses. However, among White Africans, racial endogamy tends to occur at higher rates than among Black Africans, and occurs more frequently among males than among females. When non-Arab Blacks marry US-born spouses, they also typically marry within their own race. In contrast, Black Arabs with US-born spouses are, surprisingly, more likely to have White than Black spouses, demonstrating a greater tendency to marry outside their race during the marital incorporation process. More generally, the results show that Arab Africans are more likely to marry US-born spouses from a different race than non-Arab Africans. For instance, despite their general tendency to marry US-born White spouses, White Arabs are still more likely to have US-born Black spouses than their non-Arab White counterparts.

Establishing why Black Arab Africans are more likely to marry outside their race is difficult using existing data sources. However, the social context of marriage in Arab communities points to two possibilities likely to account for this peculiarity. First, as noted in chapter 2, Arab African societies have a long history of acceptance of interracial marriages that precedes even that of the United States. Part of this reflects their greater emphasis on blood relations in determining the ancestry of mixed-race persons, in contrast to the United States, where such ancestries are determined among other things by the one-drop rule (Mazuri 1973). Second, contemporary Arab immigrants seeking potential spouses place greater emphasis on shared religious beliefs than race when making marital decisions (Naber 2005). Among Africans with US-born spouses, therefore, Arab Africans seem to be more open to marrying across their race than non-Arab African immigrants.

FIGURE 17. THE US-BORN SPOUSES OF AFRICAN MALES

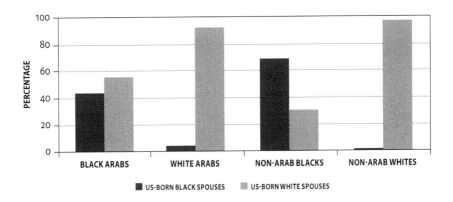

FIGURE 18. THE US-BORN SPOUSES OF AFRICAN FEMALES

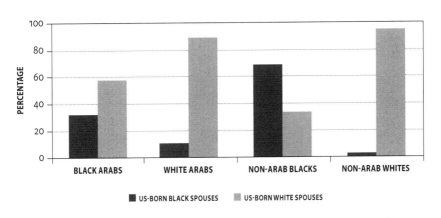

DATA SOURCE: 2006–2008 American Community Survey.

SUMMARY AND IMPLICATIONS

Marital incorporation is considered to be the best reflection of immigrants' integration into the structure of their host societies. Given its significance for understanding reductions in group differences, intermarriage between immigrants and natives provides valuable insights into the extent to which the cultural boundaries between the two groups are disappearing. As the evidence in this chapter suggests, the disappearance of these boundaries occurs in dissimilar ways across African immigrant groups. The racial and ethnic attributes of African immigrants are primary determinants of progress towards the elimination of these boundaries. Furthermore, the empirical evidence reinforces the notion that African immigrants face disparate prospects in their efforts to form intimate relationships with the US-born.

In the long run, variations in the persistence of cultural boundaries that constrain the social integration of Africans will have important implications that are differentiated across groups. For example, because racial groups with low levels of intermarriage are culturally and racially distinct from the majority of the US-born population, the speed with which they become integrated over the coming decades will be slower than that observed among groups with higher intermarriage rates.

Our understanding of the influence of race on the marital incorporation of African immigrants has, however, been clarified by three specific findings. First, White Africans marry US natives at higher rates than Black African immigrants. White Africans, therefore, find it easier than Black Africans to integrate into the institutional structure of society, insofar as marriage represents one of the major social institutions in the United States. Since marital incorporation involves transitions from origin-country to US cultural norms, the higher intermarriage rates of White Africans indicate that they have an advantage relative to Black Africans in making these transitions. Among White Africans, however, the ability to make these transitions is clearly differentiated by Arab ethnicity. Nevertheless, the primacy of race in facilitating these cultural transitions is underscored by the fact that White Arab Africans have more opportunities for forming marriages with US natives than Black Arab Africans.

Comparatively low rates of intermarriage among Black Africans, in general, are consistent with the expectation that cultural boundaries will persist for much longer between US natives and Black than White Africans. However, variations in the persistence of cultural boundaries are also likely to be observed among Black Africans. Thus, the lower intermarriage rates of Black Arab than Black non-Arab Africans raise the possibility that cultural boundaries relative to US natives will differentially decline even within the population of African immigrants with visible minority characteristics.

A second insight provided by the analysis is the observation that racial intermarriage disparities among Africans are not explained by factors such as socioeconomic status, duration of residence, and the linguistic mechanisms known to affect immigrants' fortunes in the US marriage market. Any assumption that the comparatively low average schooling levels of Black Africans explains their weaker intermarriage prospects is thus unfounded. Instead, as the analysis suggests, White Africans are still more likely to marry US-born spouses than Black Africans among immigrants with similar levels of schooling and years of US residence. Among the US-born, therefore, preferences for African spouses are not exclusively determined by factors such as levels of human capital or greater levels of acculturation. The persistence of racial intermarriage disparities after accounting for these factors supports the proposition that White Africans marry US-born spouses at higher rates than Black Africans for reasons that are not necessarily socioeconomic. This racial disparity is instead consistent with established norms influencing the use of race and ethnicity in spousal selection decisions.

Besides these mechanisms, however, the predominant tendency of Black Africans to select same-race spouses during the marital incorporation processes also exposes them to the same structural influences known to negatively affect the marital dynamics of US-born Blacks. Accordingly, declines in the availability of economically attractive males that diminish the marital chances of US-born Black females (Lichter, LeClere, and McLaughlin 1991) are also likely to affect the intermarriage prospects of Black African females. Indeed, both Black African and US-born Black females who are single draw from the same limited pool of eligible Black males in their search for potential spouses. For Black African males, the pool from which potential US-born Black spouses is selected increasingly consists of economically independent Black females who, compared to US-born White women, receive lower gains to marriage (Lichter et al. 1992). The combination of racial influences in spousal selection decisions and structural factors affecting the dynamics of Black marriages represents a formidable obstacle to the marital incorporation of Black African immigrants.

A final insight provided by the analysis is the fact that the marital incorporation process of African immigrants unfolds through mechanisms that reinforce existing racial color lines. Empirically, the analysis shows that intermarriage between Africans and the US-born largely occurs in the form of racially endogamous relationships. Furthermore, the reinforcement of racial color lines through intermarriage occurs at greater levels among White than Black African immigrants. This stems from two related processes: the higher overall levels of intermarriage among White Africans and their higher levels of racial endogamy relative to Black Africans. In the context of unequal race-relations characterized by a higher socioeconomic position of US-born Whites relative to US-born Blacks, children born to White Africans who intermarry with US-born Whites will thus be strategically positioned to maintain their high socioeconomic position across immigrant generations. Conversely, without changes to the prevailing social context, the descendants of Black Africans immigrants will be constrained by existing social and economic disadvantages associated with racial minority status and by their perceived cultural distinctiveness in relation to the broader US population.

.

Conclusion

U
S senator John Kerry married Teresa Simões-Ferreira Heinz, his second wife, in 1995. She was previously married to Henry J. Heinz III, a wealthy heir to the Henry J. Heinz company, who later died in 1991. Teresa Heinz Kerry was also a regular fixture in the US media during the 2004 presidential campaigns. While John Kerry ran as the Democratic nominee, sections of the media revived a controversial claim she made in the early 1990s. She had identified herself as an "African American" despite the fact that she is White. Heinz Kerry responded by simply pointing out that she was born in Mozambique, in southern Africa, where she lived with her Portuguese parents when it was under colonial rule. As she puts it, "my roots are African . . . the birds I remember, the fruits I ate, the trees I climbed, they're African" (Murphy 2004). Few people will nevertheless dispute the fact that she had achieved levels of social mobility that exceeded those typically observed among African immigrants. She married wealthy and powerful white men, and in so doing had been incorporated into the upper echelons of society. Before migrating to the United States, however, Teresa was part of White upper class in Mozambique. Her premigration cultural background and socioeconomic status had prepared her for a distinctively upward social trajectory after her arrival.

As African immigration to the United States increases, African-origin individuals will rise to play prominent roles in society. Teresa Heinz Kerry's role in the 2004 presidential campaign has now been surpassed by that of Barack Obama, who was elected president in 2008. Yet as the results from the preceding analyses suggest, we are less likely to see more Barack Obamas than to find more Heinz Kerrys among Africans and their descendants in the foreseeable future. In the current US racial context, it seems clear that Black African immigrants do not have the same opportunities for achieving the educational, marital, or occupational mobility that their White African counterparts have.

More generally, however, African immigrants will continue to play an important role in the changing dynamics of US immigration flows as a result of their rapid growth rates and their increasingly diverse characteristics. If current international economic and political regimes remain unchanged, they will also continue to influence the increasing trend in international migration between the global South and the global North (De Haas 2008; Kohnert 2007). African immigration to the United States will thus continue to remain important for understanding the challenges and opportunities associated with migration from less-developed to more-developed countries. At the same time, it will contribute unique dimensions of diversity to contemporary immigration movements that will add to its importance for understanding social incorporation processes. Compared to other immigrant groups, for example, African immigrants generally come from some of the world's poorest countries. They also originate from the world's largest source of Black migrant populations. This unique combination of economic and demographic characteristics creates an interesting set of dynamics in the process of African immigrant integration into Western societies. These societies are defined by their comparatively higher standards of living and multiracial demographic configurations. What happens to African immigrants in these contexts will therefore be a product of complex interactions between their distinct economic and sociocultural profiles and those of their host societies.

The analysis of how race influences the incorporation of Africans in the United States falls within this context of complex interactions. One way in which these interactions are addressed in previous studies is by the exclusive examination of the outcomes of the Black African Diaspora (e.g., Bracey 2005; Arthur 2008). While this perspective is important, the current analysis moves the discourse forward by incorporating the diverse racial and ethnic characteristics of African immigrants in the examination of their social and economic outcomes. A broader contribution of the analysis, however, is its emphasis on intra-diasporan analysis. In other words, it highlights the significance of investigating inequalities within African Diaspora populations in order to generate new insights into their social and economic circumstances.

Intra-diasporan analysis provides the principal mechanism used for underlying the central argument made in the analysis. This argument is that race and Arab ethnicity among African immigrants interact with US constructions of racial and ethnic minority status to circumscribe the pathways available to them during the incorporation process. From a historical perspective, the central argument invokes the significance of race in the incorporation of African forced-migrant populations in the United States. In particular, negative constructions of race and their association with Blackness between the seventeenth and nineteenth centuries undergirded the exploitation of Black Africans during the period of slavery (Jordan 1968; Wilson 1996). Nevertheless, the analysis also offers a new perspective for understanding the dynamics of more contemporary racial influences on the incorporation of recent African immigrants. As shown in the preceding chapters, the influence of race on the outcomes of contemporary Africans has clearly evolved.

An important dimension of this evolution is the integration of the racial diversity found among African immigrants into a system of barriers and rewards. One defining feature of this system is that it influences the welfare of African immigrants by the degree of correspondence between their race and US racial hierarchies. Also related to the evolution is the interaction between the race of African immigrants and their ethnic differences to produce even more differentiated patterns of social inequality. Studies among non-African immigrant groups have shown similar interactions and their contributions to inequalities among White (Alba, Logan, and Crowder 1997) and Black immigrants (Thomas 2011b) more generally. In the context of racial influences among African immigrants, Arab ethnicity is an important mediator of intraracial inequalities. Yet Arab-origin Africans, a key segment of the African immigrant population, are missing in many studies on the African Diaspora in the United States. As this analysis suggests, however, Arab Africans confront a range of cultural and religious stereotypes that affect their welfare. These stereotypes seem to be considerably differentiated from those confronted by non-Arab African immigrants.

The focus on Arab ethnicity as a basis for understanding social inequalities is admittedly limited since it understates the ethnic diversity found among African populations. Notwithstanding this limitation, however, few will dispute the growing significance of Arab ethnicity in the post–September 11, 2001, US social context. Since Arab ethnicity is the principal sociocultural distinction found among White Africans, distinguishing between the outcomes of Arab and non-Arab Whites is also important. In general, this helps to demonstrate that the advantages associated with Whiteness among Africans are not necessarily consistent across groups. In general, the realities of contemporary US society and the growing number of Arab Africans migrating to the United States suggest that the distinction between Arabs and non-Arabs is among the most important ethnic distinction affecting the incorporation of Africans.

THEORETICAL IMPLICATIONS

Instructively, the inequalities found among African immigrants in the analysis have a number of theoretical implications. The first of these is that they provide an implicit connection between the patterns of racial inequality found within the African immigrant population and corresponding patterns of racial inequality found in Africa. Thus, although understated in previous studies, race appears to have cross-continental implications for access to resources and group socioeconomic position among African-born populations. Its specific influence is likely to vary across continental contexts. However, because the analysis largely focuses on Africans in the United States, it provides limited empirical basis for examining the comparative influence of race in the United States and African origin societies. Racial inequalities in Africa nevertheless have an indirect influence on the outcomes for African immigrants after their arrival, although these impacts are largely intuitive. For example, White Africans, on average, have greater access to socioeconomic resources than Black Africans before migration and are thus likely to arrive with greater levels of financial and human capital. At the point of arrival, therefore, African immigrants have inequalities in endowments, conditional on race, which could by themselves result in differential patterns of social mobility.

Beyond these initial differences, however, the US social context has an additional influence on racial inequalities among African immigrants. At the very least, it creates an environment in which premigration racial differences are allowed to persist. At the same time, the lingering stratification patterns found during the incorporation process raise the possibility that it further accentuates racial inequalities among Africans irrespective of their initial differences in human-capital endowments. White Africans, for example, have higher occupational status and earnings than Black Africans among individuals with similar levels of schooling. Rewards to postimmigration acculturation are likewise racially differentiated since English proficiency, for example, is associated with larger socioeconomic rewards among White than Black African immigrants.

Racial variations in the social and economic incorporation of Africans are therefore inconsistent with conventional theories predicting ubiquitous patterns of social mobility during the incorporation process. More relevant for understanding the diverse pathways available to African immigrants are theories that integrate racial and ethnic differences into their explanatory frameworks. In line with segmented assimilation theory, for example, the opportunities and constraints encountered by African immigrants are considerably differentiated on the basis of race. Each racial pathway found among Africans is further differentiated by Arab ethnicity, resulting in at least four broad patterns of social mobility. Additionally, the consistently less favorable social and economic outcomes found among Black Africans further support Bashi and McDaniel's (1997) argument that Black immigrants are incorporated into the bottom of the US racial hierarchy. As they suggest, the racial constraints faced by Black African immigrants are rooted in the broad social construction of Blackness and its related consequence of systematic exposure to prejudice and discrimination. In short, the systematic disadvantage of race is a barrier to the social mobility of Black populations in the United States irrespective of whether they are immigrants or US natives.

These findings further provide a nuanced understanding of the dynamics of racial stratification processes and their relevance for understanding inequalities. Specifically, they move us beyond the dichotomous distinction between Blacks and Whites and its associated implications. In the process, they contribute to a more polytomous understanding of racial stratification, at least among African immigrants. In place of the three-tier hierarchy proposed by Bonilla-Silva (2004), however, a four-tiered hierarchy emerges from the analysis. As expected, non-Arab Whites are consistently found at the top of the hierarchy, followed by White Arabs, non-Arab Blacks, and Black Arabs. Among African immigrants, therefore, simply having White or Black racial characteristics does not determine what stratum of society subgroups occupy. Apart from racial attributes, the presence or absence of a perceived ethnic-minority disadvantage is also important for determining a group's socioeconomic position, especially at the polar ends of the racial stratification hierarchy.

A final theoretical contribution of the analysis is that it provides clarity to scholarly debates concerning whether or not Arab immigrants have a unique experience that warrants their classification into a separate racial category (e.g., Gold 2004). Based on the empirical evidence presented in these analyses, we can conclude that Arab immigrants do indeed have different experiences compared to non-Arab immigrants. Still, the findings clearly underscore the fact that Black Arabs face different socioeconomic realities than their White Arab counterparts.

Along with Arab racial variations documented in the literature (Al-Khatib 2006; Fabos 2008; Nigem 1986) therefore, the findings undermine the conceptual case for classifying Arab immigrants into a distinct racial group. As a result, interactions between race and Arab ethnicity should be considered in research on the incorporation processes of Arab-origin populations.

REVISITING THE DISCOURSE ON BLACK IMMIGRANT SUCCESS

Beyond their theoretical relevance, the results also contribute to the discourse on the apparent success of Black immigrants in the United States. In particular, they undermine claims of an extraordinary pattern of success among Black Africans and reject the notion that they are a new model minority group. This argument is generally consistent with those made in prior studies on Black immigrants from the Caribbean (e.g., Model 1991; 1995). However, in contrast to these previous studies, which focus on specific outcomes (e.g., labor force outcomes), a more comprehensive challenge to the Black immigrant success narrative emerges in the preceding chapters. For example, the findings consistently challenge the narrative by using multiple socioeconomic indicators to demonstrate that Black Africans have suboptimal attainment levels compared to White Africans. In doing so, they also directly undermine the presumption that Black immigrants have surmounted the barrier of racial minority status that typically constricts the social mobility of US-born Blacks.

Invalidating the narrative of Black immigrant success does not, however, imply that Black Africans experience no improvements in their welfare as a result of their migration to the United States. Despite the racial challenges they encounter, many Black Africans have better living conditions in the United States than in their origin countries. Black African refugees, for example, generally live in more secure contexts as result of their migration to the United States in comparison to the life-threatening circumstances they faced before migration. Incomes and living standards are also generally higher in the United States than in Africa, allowing Africans immigrants to remit millions of dollars to their origin countries each year. By and large, these unquestionably positive consequences must be considered in the broader evaluation of the consequences of African migration to the United States. Nevertheless, they should not distract us from the social imperative of providing equal access to opportunity for all immigrants; an ideal that guides the process of socioeconomic achievement after immigrants arrive on US shores.

Policy Implications

If the end goal of the social incorporation of immigrants is to make them productive citizens, it seems clear that African immigrants are making differential rates of progress toward this ideal. Summary measures of their educational and economic well-being therefore provide an incomplete basis for developing the kinds of policies needed to improve their well-being. Consequently, the process of improving the welfare of disadvantaged African immigrants must begin by acknowledging the significance of race in creating barriers to social mobility during the incorporation process. This proposition, however, seems deceptively obvious. Yet if policymakers conflate the outcomes of all African immigrants with those of Black Africans, they will inadvertently underemphasize the degree of disadvantage faced by the latter. For example, because Black African incomes are lower than those of White Africans, the average poverty rates of all African immigrants conceal the true extent of the economic disadvantage found in Black African immigrant families. By decomposing the social indicators of African immigrants into their racially constituent parts, policymakers will become less prone to the influence of the initial picture presented by these averages. The use of racially differentiated indicators will also correctly inform commentators lauding Black Africans' presumed ability to overcome the disadvantage of race. Ending such commentaries will also cease to distract us from the obvious need to address the acute social inequalities found in African immigrant subgroups.

With regard to the specific disadvantages encountered by Black African families, a number of existing policies can be used in order to improve outcomes. Resources are available to low-income Black African families who meet the eligibility requirements of Head Start programs to help them improve the educational, health, and nutrition outcomes of their children. Many immigrants in such families are also likely to meet the eligibility requirements of related programs (e.g., Temporary Assistance to Needy Families—TANF) and thus qualify for additional types of assistance. Given the relative recency of contemporary Black African immigration, however, the existence of these programs does not by itself indicate that they will effectively contribute to the reduction of racial inequalities. For these reductions to happen an additional step needs to be taken in the form of creating new strategies designed to increase the participation rates of eligible African immigrant families in these existing programs.

Policies addressing educational inequalities can likewise be utilized to tackle the race-related schooling disadvantages found among African immigrant youths. Slower rates of schooling progress among Black than White African immigrant youths need to be addressed in order to avoid their long-term nega-tive consequences for enrollment in postsecondary institutions. Affirmative action policies are, however, unlikely to provide a practical basis for addressing the educational disadvantage of Black African youth. In part, this is due to the fact that despite their educational disadvantage in comparison to White African youths, Black Africans are generally *less* disadvantaged in terms of schooling than are US-born Black youth. In addition, despite the similarities in the racial disadvantages faced by Black Africans and US-born Blacks, the latter are the spe-cific group around which affirmation action policies were originally developed (Skrentny 2001). Policymakers can, however, exploit other available opportuni-ties in order to reduce racial schooling inequalities among African youth. Within schools, for example, the outcomes of Black African youth could be improved by expanded attention to the needs of English as a second language (ESL) learners and the elimination of teacher stereotypes about Black students, both of which can affect the achievement of minority youth.

In terms of occupational attainment, differences in the rewards to foreign and domestic schooling among African immigrants provide unique opportunities for policy intervention. Occupational disadvantages associated with foreign schooling credentials point to a need for more effective credential validation policies to help employers evaluate credentials obtained abroad. Moreover, the advantage associated with having US credentials provides a significant rationale for creating opportunities for acquiring additional accreditation after the arrival of new immigrants. Without these interventions, foreign-educated Africans, especially those who are Black or Arab, will continue to find it difficult to utilize their human capital to improve the welfare of their families.

Cultural and religious stereotypes associated with Arab ethnicity are more complex issues that need to be addressed by policymakers. As the analysis suggests, these stereotypes are constraints to socioeconomic mobility among Arab-Africans irrespective of their racial attributes. Consequently, the status quo, in which presumed religious markers associated with Arab names and Islamic-related attire disproportionately constrict the mobility of Arab immigrants, cannot be sustained without having negative long-term implications. Ingenious strategies will therefore need to be developed to prevent these stereotypes from limiting the ability of Arab-origin Africans to become productive citizens.

Possibilities for Future Research

Expanding research on African immigrants will require comprehensive future studies that further illuminate the dynamics of their social incorporation processes. A major obstacle to this enterprise, however, is the lack of extensive data on the outcomes of African immigrants. Traditional census-based data sources, such as those used in these analyses, continue to be a useful alternative information source in the absence of more extensive data sources. Nevertheless, they are limited for answering the wider range of questions future studies need to address. Census-related data sources, for example, lack information on African immigrants' motivations for migration, their premigration social characteristics, and their indicators of psychological well-being. This information needs to be collected and analyzed in future studies. Essential qualitative data complementing information from quantitative data sources are also very limited. Thus, the expansion of both the quantitative and qualitative data sources used in research on African immigrants is central to the development of more extensive future studies.

Future studies should also use longitudinal perspectives to better understand African immigration processes, in general, and the long-term impacts of the determinants of intra-African social inequalities. Compared to cross-sectional studies, longitudinal analyses can provide a more comprehensive perspective on a number of social processes. For example, they can be used to improve our understanding of how lived experiences in multiracial contexts prior to migration shape the postmigration circumstances of African immigrants. Such studies can be used to track explicit changes in the outcomes of Black and White Africans that occurred between the premigration and postmigration periods. Another advantage of using longitudinal studies is that they are useful for determining whether or not motivations for migration vary among White and Black Africans and whether these variations have implications for subsequent occupational, marital, or educational incorporation processes. Refugee immigration, for example, may be a more important motivation for Black African migration, while the search for employment may be more important for White Africans. Prior to migration, both groups may also vary in terms of whether they are motivated by the pursuit of temporary rather than permanent migration. A specific contribution of such longitudinal studies is that they can help us understand whether racial differences in migration motivations result in group differences in subsequent social investments in the United States that may in turn influence occupational or intermarriage differences.

Very little is also known about the dynamics of prejudice and discrimination encountered by African immigrants and their reactions to these dynamics. Future studies should thus articulate these dynamics while highlighting their influence on subsequent patterns of inequality. Research indicates, for example, that prior experience of discrimination is major predictor of perceptions of risk and vulnerability (Satterfield, Mertz, and Slovic 2004). Whites, who have the least exposure to prejudice and discrimination, thus tend to be less risk averse than non-Whites (Rosen, Tsai, and Downs 2003). Among African immigrants, therefore, initial experiences with prejudice and discrimination are likely to have significant long-term implications for racial inequalities. For example, prior studies will suggest that initial encounters with racism will negatively affect Black immigrants' willingness to explore more rewarding opportunities. Conversely, experiences signaling a presumed advantage associated with Whiteness are likely to help White Africans feel less restricted than Black Africans in the pursuit of more rewarding opportunities for social mobility.

Future studies also need to address the question of how racial inequalities among Africans are transmitted across immigrant generations. Much of the recent increase in research on African immigrants has been driven by studies on the outcomes of foreign-born or first-generation Africans. As a result, there is limited scholarly focus on immigrants in the second or later generations. Studies on the dynamics of race across generations can be used to reach more definitive conclusions regarding the long-term influence of race on assimilation trajectories. With recent increases in African immigration, however, a more immediate concern is the examination of how the constraint of racial minority status affects the well-being of the children of African immigrants, that is, second-generation immigrants. Studies clarifying these racial influences should also analyze the welfare of second-generation children born in interracial unions between Africans and the US-born. Among other things, this will help us understand the ways in which multiracial identities influence the assimilation of second-generation African children.

More generally, studies on racial and ethnic identification processes are integral to any comprehensive future research agenda on African immigrants. While fixed US racial constructs are important for understanding patterns of social inequality, they have limited import for showing how nontraditional constructions of race affect the welfare of African immigrants. Despite their lighter skin tones, for example, South African immigrants who identify themselves as "Colored" fall under the predominant US social construction of Blackness. Nevertheless, it is not clear whether they have different reactions to the barriers associated with racial minority status than their comparatively darker-skinned Black African counterparts. Another relevant issue to be examined in future studies is the identity formation processes of non-Arab White Africans. How do immigrants such as Teresa Heinz Kerry identify themselves, and how do these identities fit into the sociopolitical boundaries of racial group membership? If systematic constructions of racial-ethnic identities are absent among non-Arab Whites, this may have broader implications that suggest that they have particularly rapid rates of assimilation into the White majority. Differential constructions of race and identity may also have further implications for understanding inequalities among Arab immigrants. The current analysis, highlighting inequalities among Arabs who identify themselves at opposite ends of the racial spectrum, provides an important first step that could be expanded in future studies. As noted in prior studies, the identity formation processes of Arab immigrants are more complex and may even involve the use of multiple identity schemas (Ajrouch and Jamal 2007; Wingfield 2006).

Furthermore, despite the significance of the Arab/non-Arab ethnic dichotomy for understanding inequalities among African immigrants, larger configurations of ethnicity may also influence their social incorporation processes. These configurations are generally more extensive among Black Africans, and as prior research suggests, the social and economic outcomes of Black African immigrants have unique manifestations across ethnic groups (Perry 1997; Kasirye 2008; Reynolds 2002). Clearly, the vast plurality of African ethnicities makes it impractical to conduct separate analysis of each immigrant ethnic group. Nevertheless, more extensive information on ethnic differences can be incorporated by future studies, especially in those attempting to determine how ethnic differences drive inequalities among African immigrant populations.

Notwithstanding the favorable socioeconomic outcomes observed among White African immigrants, there is also limited research examining whether they have better or worse trajectories of social mobility than other White immigrants. Future research on the African Diaspora can therefore be expanded by investigating whether there are implications of having African origins associated with differential incorporation experiences among White African and White non-African immigrants. Differences in premigration contexts may be important in this regard. For example, while White Africans have higher standards of living than Blacks in African societies, they still originate from countries that are for the most part less developed than the origin countries of White European immigrants. Studies examining these implications are important and will further contribute to the understanding of how Africans abroad are incorporated into Western social stratification schemes.

Data and Methods Used in the Analysis

R eliable and representative information on the social and economic characteristics of African immigrants is lacking in most US data sets. Consequently, in order to empirically describe racial and ethnic differences in the outcomes of African immigrants, the analysis employs data from the 2006–2008 American Community Survey (ACS). These data are produced by the US Census Bureau. They were developed in an attempt to phase out the use of questions on issues such as place of birth, marital status, and incomes that were previously asked in long-forms questionnaires in decennial US population censuses. Since 2000, the ACS has become the primary source of representative information on the social and economic characteristics of the US population. The limited availability of alternative data on African immigrants further underscores the utility of the ACS data as the most comprehensive source of information on their demographic and socioeconomic attributes. Data from the ACS are thus useful because they provide information on a range of characteristics, including respondents' age and sex, as well as their economic, occupational, and marital characteristics.

Identifying Race and Ethnicity among Africans

Using ACS data on place of birth, the analysis defines African immigrants as individuals who were born in an African country. Furthermore, information on race is used to identify Black and White African-born individuals who currently live in the United States. A major advantage associated with using information from the ACS is the fact it allows respondents to give self-reported information on their ethnic and ancestral origins. In short, information on race used in the analysis refers to how Africans racially identified themselves in the ACS data. Race and ancestral information is useful for identifying the population in a range of ethnicities. Although respondents were allowed to give as many ancestries as possible, the ACS data only report their first and second responses. Information on these ethnic ancestries is therefore used to capture individuals who identify themselves as Arabs. As scholars such as Nigem (1986) and Read (2004) maintain, Arabs are typically identified in such data sets as individuals who trace any of their ancestries to an Arab country.

Race and ancestry information is subsequently used to distinguish between Black and White Africans who have Arab and non-Arab ethnic ancestries. Accordingly, non-Arab Black Africans are defined as non-Arab Africans who identify themselves as Black. Non-Arab White Africans are similarly defined as Africans who identify themselves as White but have a non-Arab ethnic origin. Africans with Arab ethnic origins are also differentiated as Black Arabs and White Arabs, depending on their race. Altogether, these four groups account for about 94 percent of all African immigrants in the data used in the analysis. The majority of these were non-Arab Blacks (64 percent), followed by non-Arab Whites (14.9 percent), White Arabs (12.9 percent), and Black Arabs (2 percent). Significantly, although the proportional contribution of Black Arabs is the smallest, as suggested in chapter 2, there are important conceptual and historical reasons for including them in the analysis. Among African immigrants, there is also a residual category of "other" Africans who account for about 6.2 percent of the total population. This category of "other" Africans includes Africans who identify themselves using other non-Black and non-White racial categories.

EDUCATIONAL OUTCOMES

Data from the ACS also provide information on selected educational outcomes (e.g., educational attainment and current school enrollment). This information is used in two ways to examine the educational outcomes of African immigrants. First, information on educational attainment is used to examine the percentage distribution of Africans in various completed levels of schooling. These estimates are reported for adults age twenty-five and above in chapter 3. Second, the analysis uses information on both the highest completed level of schooling and current school enrollment, in order to examine differences in schooling progress among currently enrolled youths. The specific outcome of interest in this case is the expected grade for age among high-school-age youths. In line with previous studies (e.g., Deming and Dynarski 2008; Hauser, Simmons, and Pager 2000), expected grade for age is defined as the modal grade level completed by individuals in each specific age.

Racial and ethnic differences in the likelihood of completing the expected grade for age among African high-school-age immigrant youths are generally examined using logistic regression models estimated using data for individuals between age fifteen and seventeen. The basic form of the model used in the analysis is presented below.

$$E_{ij} = \alpha_{ij} + \beta R_{ij} + \beta A_{ij} + \beta F_{ij} + \beta Im_{ij} + \epsilon \quad (1)$$

The dependent variable, E_{ij}, estimates the odds of achieving the expected grade for age for child i in household j. The independent variables include R_{ij}, their race and ethnicity; A_{ij}, demographic characteristics such as age and sex; F_{ij}, family income; and Im_{ij}, a collection of immigration-related characteristics such as duration of residence, level of English proficiency, and country of origin. Models examining differences among children with only US schooling are also estimated using data for children in between ages fifteen and seventeen who arrived in the United States before age six.

Occupational Outcomes

The analysis of the occupational outcomes of African immigrants is restricted to individuals between ages twenty-five and sixty-four. It also focuses on two sets of occupational attainment outcomes: an overall measure of occupational prestige and education-occupation mismatches. With regard to the former, existing studies use a number of indicators, including Duncan's Socioeconomic Index (SEI) and the Standard International Occupational Prestige Scale, to measure levels of occupational prestige. Duncan's SEI measures occupational attainment using the income and educational level associated with each occupation, based on an occupational classification system developed in 1950. This index has been widely used in studies on the relationship between migration processes and occupational attainment (e.g., Alderman and Tolnay 2003; Akresh 2006; Tolnay 2001; Hirschman and Wong 1984). Hauser and Warren (1997), however, argue that the Standard International Occupational Prestige Scale used in previous studies lacks criterion validity. Consequently, they developed a new SEI that updates the Duncan index using the US census's 1990 occupational classification system. This new index, or the Hauser and Warren SEI, is the first outcome used to examine race-ethnic differences in occupational attainment among African immigrants.

OLS regression models are thus used to describe how factors such as racial and ethnic differences are associated with overall levels of occupational attainment. The basic form of the estimation model used in the regression analysis is presented below.

$$lnHWSEI = \alpha + \beta R + \beta A + \beta H + \beta W + \beta M + \epsilon \quad (2)$$

The dependent variable is the log transformation of the Hauser and Warrant SEI since this transformation facilitates the interpretation of the estimated coefficients for the independent variables. R measures racial and ethnic characteristics; A is a vector of individual demographic characteristics, such as age and sex; while H represents levels of schooling. The model also uses information on age and completed years of schooling to generate proxy estimates of work experience W. However, estimates of the work experience coefficients were not associated with occupational status as expected. This may be due to the difficulties involved in distinguishing between pre- and postmigration work experience. Finally, Model 2 includes M, representing several migration-related attributes among Africans, including country of origin, duration of residence, and whether or not individuals are English-proficient. Model 2 is also estimated using data for highly educated African immigrants, that is, those with at least a bachelor's degree, to examine occupational disparities among foreign- and US-educated individuals.

Distinguishing between Foreign- and US-Educated Immigrants

Analyzing the occupational returns to university education earned from either foreign countries or the United States requires specific types of premigration information not currently available in the ACS data. However, following Mattoo, Neagu, and Ozden (2008), a proxy indicator is used to determine where immigrants in the sample are most likely to have received their schooling. Specifically, data on immigrants' age at arrival and their highest level of schooling are therefore used to distinguish between US- and foreign-educated immigrants. Accordingly, US-educated individuals are identified as immigrants who arrived in the United States at an age before which one would typically be expected to complete the person's stated highest level of schooling. Using this strategy, for example, individuals who currently have a bachelor's degree but arrived in the United States at age twelve are considered to be US-educated. Conversely, those with a similar degree who arrived at age sixty are considered to be foreign-educated. Since this method is likely to be biased if used to determine where noncollege graduates received their schooling, comparisons of the occupational outcomes of foreign- and US-educated Africans are only conducted for individuals with at least an undergraduate degree.

Education-Occupation Mismatch Status

The second set of occupational outcomes examined in the analysis is the mismatch between educational attainment and occupational status. This strategy has been used in a number of studies (e.g., Chiswick and Miller 2010; Quinn and Rubb 2005) to examine the extent to which educational credentials are appropriately utilized in the labor market. In general, individuals are considered to be mismatched if they have either more or less education than the norm in their current occupations. Three groups of education-occupation mismatches are thus identified. Correct matches involve individuals with the normative schooling levels in the occupations; overeducated workers, those who have more than the normative schooling levels; and undereducated workers, with less than the normative schooling level in their occupations.

Standard approaches used to examine education-occupation mismatch status include expert job assessments (Vaisey 2006), worker self-assessments (Duncan and Hoffman 1981), and realized matching procedures (Chiswick and Miller 2010). In realized matching procedures, for example, the mean plus one standard deviation (SD) of educational attainment of workers within a specific occupation, or the modal level of schooling within occupations, is used to identify correct matches (i.e., normative levels of education). Workers with more and less than these normative levels of schooling are considered to be over- and undereducated respectively. Although estimates from both realized matching procedures are generally similar, some scholars (e.g., Cohn and Khan 1995) argue that modal matching procedures provide more precise estimates than estimates derived from the mean-plus-one-SD matching procedure.

Information on educational attainment and occupational status available in the ACS facilitates the use of realized mismatching procedures in the analysis. As a result, the normative level of schooling for each occupation is defined as the modal year of schooling among all workers in that occupation. In other words, these norms are determined using schooling information for all workers in the United States employed in each occupation. Overeducated and undereducated individuals are then respectively defined as individuals who have more or less than the normative level of schooling in each occupation.

EARNINGS

As in the examination of occupational outcomes, analysis of earnings differences focuses on individuals between ages twenty-five and sixty-four. Multiple regression analysis of the determinants of earnings differences particularly focuses on differences in hourly wages. Earnings differences are thus estimated as

$$lnE = \alpha + \beta R + \beta A + \beta H + \beta M + \epsilon, \quad (3)$$

where the dependent variable lnE is the log of African immigrants' hourly wages. R measures racial and ethnic characteristics, A demographic characteristics such as age and sex, *H* levels of schooling, and *M* migration-related attributes such as country of origin, duration of residence, and whether or not individuals are English-proficient. This model is also used to examine earning disparities among the self-employed and among foreign- and US-educated Africans.

MARITAL STATUS

Data on African immigrants ages eighteen and above are used in the analysis of intermarriage patterns among African immigrants. Information on the nativity status of the spouses of adult African immigrants is used to capture the main outcome of interest, that is, whether or not they have a US-born spouse. Accordingly, African immigrants are considered to have intermarried with US natives if their spouses indicated that they were born in the United States. Two methodological approaches are typically used in regression analysis of intermarriage; log-linear analysis (e.g., Qian and Lichter 2001) and logistic regression analysis (e.g., Bean and Stevens 2003; Jacobs and Labov 2002). The analysis opts for the latter since, among other things, its associated estimates, expressed as odds ratios, are easier to interpret. Focusing on the outcomes of married African immigrants, disparities in the odds of intermarriage are thus analyzed as follows:

$$IM = \alpha + \beta R + \beta A + \beta H + \beta M + \epsilon, \quad (4)$$

where *IM*, the dependent variable, represents the odds of intermarriage to a US-born spouse among married Africans. These odds are considered to be a function of *R*, the racial and ethnic characteristics of African immigrants; *A*, their age; *E*, their highest level of educational attainment; and *M*, their migration-related characteristics such as duration of residence, language proficiency, and country of origin. As in previous studies (e.g., Kulczycki and Lobo 2002; Jacobs and Labov 2002), separate estimates are derived for males and females. This also facilitates the assessment of the unique contribution of social and economic factors to determinants of intermarriage among males and females.

References

Abu-Laban, S., and Abu-Laban, B. (1999). "Teens Between: The Public and Private Spheres of Arab Canadian Adolescents." In *Arabs in America: Building a New Future*, edited by M. W. Suleiman, 114–128. Philadelphia, PA: Temple University Press.

Adepoju, A. (1991). "South-North Migration: The African Experience." *International Migration Review*, 29: 205–221.

Agbajoh-Laoye, G. O. (2006). "Lifting the Yoke of Tradition: African Market-Women Diaspora: From Kaneshie, Accra to Harlem, New York." In *The New African Diaspora in North America*, edited by B. K. Takyi and K. Konadu-Agyemang, 235–256. Lanham, MD: Rowman and Littlefield.

Ainsworth-Darnell, J. W., and Downey, D. B. (1998). "Assessing the Oppositional Culture Explanation for Racial/Ethnic Differences in School Performance." *American Sociological Review*, 63(4): 536–553.

Ajrouch, K. J., and Jamal, A. A. (2007). "Assimilating to a White Identity: The Case of Arab Americans." International Migration Review, 41(4): 860–879.

Akresh, I. R. (2006). "Occupational Mobility among Legal Immigrants to the United States." *International Migration Review*, 40(4): 854–884.

Akresh, I. R. (2008). "Occupational Trajectories of Legal US Immigrants: Downgrading and Recovery." *Population and Development Review*, 34(3): 435–456.

Alba, R. D., Logan, J. R., and Crowder, K. (1997). "White Ethnic Neighborhood Assimilation: The Greater New York Region, 1980 to 1990." *Social Forces*, 75(3): 883–912.

Alba, R. D., and Nee, V. (1997). "Rethinking Assimilation Theory for a New Era of Immigration." *International Migration Review*, 31(4): 826–874.

Alderman, H., Orazem, P. F., and Paterno, E. M. (2001). "School Quality, School Cost, and the Public/ Private School Choices of Low Income Households In Pakistan." *Journal of Human Resources*, 36(2): 304–326.

Alderman, R. M., and Tolnay, S. T. (2003). "Occupational Status among Immigrants and African-Americans at the Beginning and End of the Great Migration." *Sociological Perspectives*, 46(2): 179–206.

Al-Khatib, M. (2006). "Aspects of Bilingualism in the Arab World: An Introduction." *International Journal of Bilingual Education*, 9(1): 1–6.

Arthur, J. A. (2000). *Invisible Sojourners: African Immigrant Diasporas in the US*. Westport, CT: Praeger.

Arthur, J. A. (2008). *The African Diaspora in the United States and Europe: The Ghanaian Experience*. London: Ashgate.

Assali, A., Khamaysi, N., and Birnbaum, Y. (1997). "Juvenile ECG Pattern in Adult Black Arabs." *Journal of Electrocardiology*, 30(2): 87–90.

Austin, R. (1994). "'An Honest Living': Street Vendors, Municipal Regulation, and the Black Public Sphere." *Yale Law Journal*, 103(8): 2119–2131.

Aynte, A. (2007). "African Immigrants Sue Minority Owned Transportation Company." *Minnesota Independent*, January 1.

Babou, C. A. (2002). "Brotherhood Solidarity, Education and Migration: The Role of the *Dahiras* among the Murid Muslim Community of New York." *African Affairs*, 101(403): 151–170.

Babou, C. A. (2008). "Migration and Cultural Change: Money, 'Caste,' Gender, and Social Status among Senegalese Female Hair Braiders in the United States." *Africa Today*, 55(2): 3–22.

Bashi, V., and McDaniel, A. (1997). "A Theory of Immigration and Racial Stratification." *Journal of Black Studies*, 27(5): 668–682.

Bassett, T. J. (1994). "Cartography and Empire Building in Nineteenth-Century West Africa." *Geographical Journal*, 84(3): 316–335.

Batson, C. D., Qian, Z., and Lichter, D. T. (2006). "Interracial and Intraracial Patterns of Mate Selection among America's Diverse Black Populations." *Journal of Marriage and the Family*, 68(3): 658–672.

Bayoumi, M. (2008). *How Does It Feel to Be a Problem?: Being Young and Arab in America*. New York, NY: Penguin Press.

Bean, F., Lee, J., Batalova, J., and Leach, M. (2005). "Immigration and Fading Color Lines in America." In *The American People: Census 2000*, edited by R. Farley and J. Haaga, 302–331. New York, NY: Russell Sage Foundation.

Bean, F., and Stevens, G. (2003). *America's Newcomers and the Dynamics of Diversity*. New York, NY: Russell Sage Foundation.

Becker, G. S. (1962). "Investment in Human Capital: A Theoretical Analysis." *Journal of Political Economy*, 70(5): 9–49.

Bender, L. M. (1983). "Color Term Encoding in a Special Lexical Domain: Sudanese Arabic Skin." *Anthropological Linguistics*, 25(1): 19–27.

Berman, B. (1984). "Structure and Process in the Bureaucratic States of Colonial Africa." *Development and Change*, 15(2): 161–202.

Bersudskaya, V., and Cataldi, E. F. (2011). *Public High School Teachers of Career and Technical Education in 2007–2008: Web Tables*. US Department of Education, National Center for Education Statistics (NCES) 2011-235.

Blau, P. M., Blum, T. C., and Schwartz, J. E. (1982). "Heterogeneity and Intermarriage." *American Sociological Review*, 47(1): 45–62.

Bonilla-Silva, E. (2002). "Where Is the Love? A Rejoinder by Bonilla-Silva on the Latin Americanization Thesis." *Race and Society*, 5(1): 103–114.

Bonilla-Silva, E. (2004). "From Bi-racial to Tri-racial: Towards a New System of Racial Stratification in the USA." *Ethnic and Racial Studies*, 27(6): 931–950.

Boone, J. L., and Benco, N. L. (1999). "Islamic Settlement in North Africa and the Iberian Peninsula." *Annual Review of Anthropology*, 28: 51–71.

Boswell, R. A. (2003). "Racism and U.S. Immigration Law: Prospects for Reform after 9/11." *Immigration and Nationality Law Review*, 24: 65–106.

Boyd, M., and Thomas, D. (2002). "Skilled Immigrant Labour: Country of Origin and the Occupational Locations of Male Engineers." *Canadian Studies in Population*, 29(1): 71–99.

Bracey, E. N. (2005). *Places in Political Time: Voices from the Black Diaspora*, Lanham, MD: University Press of America.

Bratsberg, B., and Ragan, J. F. (2002). "The Impact of Host-Country Schooling on Earnings." *Journal of Human Resources*, 37(1): 63–105.

Brittingham A., and De la Cruz, G. (2005). "We the People of Arab Ancestry in the United States." *Census 2000 Special Reports*, CENSR-21.

Bushman, B. J., and Bonacci, A. M. (2004). "You've Got Mail: Using E-mail to Examine the Effect of Prejudiced Attitudes on Discrimination against Arabs." *Journal of Experimental Social Psychology*, 40: 753–759.

Butcher, K. F. (1994). "Black Immigrants in the United States: A Comparison with Native Blacks and Other Immigrants." *Industrial and Labor Relations Review*, 47(2): 265–284.

Capps, R., McCabe, K., and Fix, M. (2011). *New Streams: Black African Migration to the United States*. Washington, DC: Migration Policy Institute.

Carliner, G. (2000). "The Language Ability of U.S. Immigrants: Assimilation and Cohort Effects." *International Migration Review*, 34(1): 158–182.

Chacko, E. (2003). "Identity and Assimilation among Young Ethiopian Immigrants in Metropolitan Washington." *Geographical Review*, 93(4): 491–506.

Charara, H. (2000). "Eight Houses from the Birthplace of Henry Ford." In *Arab Detroit: From Margin to Mainstream*, edited by N. Abraham and A. Shryock, 45–48. Detroit, MI: Wayne State University Press.

Chege, M. (1997). "Africans of European Descent." *Transition*, 73: 74–86.

Chiswick, B. R., and Miller, P. W. (2002). "Immigrant Earnings: Language Skills, Linguistic Concentrations and the Business Cycle." *Journal of Population Economics*, 15(1): 31–57.

Chiswick, B. R., and Miller, P. W. (2008). "Why Is the Payoff to Schooling Smaller for Immigrants?" *Labour Economics*, 15(6): 1317–1340.

Chiswick, B. R., and Miller, P. W. (2010). "The International Transferability of Human Capital." *Economics of Education Review*, 28: 162–169.

Cohn, E., and Khan, S. (1995). "The Wage Effects of Overschooling Revisited." *Labour Economics*, 2(1): 67–76.

Crush, J. (2002). "The Global Raiders: Nationalism, Globalization and the South African Brain Drain." *Journal of International Affairs*, 56(1): 147–172.

Daneshvary, N., and Schwer, R. K. (1994). "Black Immigrants in the U.S. Labor Market: An Earnings Analysis." *Review of Black Political Economy*, 22(3): 77–98.

Daniels, R. (2004). *Guarding the Golden Door: American Immigration Policy and Immigrants since 1882*. New York, NY: Hill and Wang.

Danso, R. K., and Grant, M. R. (2000). "Access to Housing as an Adaptive Strategy for Immigrant Groups: Africans in Calgary." *Canadian Ethnic Studies*, 32(3): 19–43.

Darity, W. A., and Mason, P. L. (1998). "Evidence on Discrimination in Employment: Codes of Color, Codes of Gender." *Journal of Economic Perspectives*, 12(2): 63–90.

Dávila, A., and Mora, M. T. (2004). "English-Language Skills and the Earnings of Self-Employed Immigrants in the United States: A Note." *Industrial Relations: A Journal of Economy and Society*, 43(2): 386–391.

Dávila, A., and Mora, T. M. (2005). "Changes in the Earnings of Arab Men in the US between 2000 and 2002." *Journal of Population Economics*, 18(4): 587–601.

Dee, T. S. (2004). "Teachers, Race, and Student Achievement in a Randomized Experiment." *Review of Economics and Statistics*, 86(1): 195–210.

DeHaas, H. (2008). "The Myth of Invasion: The Inconvenient Realities of African Migration to Europe." *Third World Quarterly*, 29(7): 1305–1322.

De la Cruz, G. P., and Brittingham, A. (2003). *The Arab Population: 2000*. Washington, DC: U.S. Census Bureau.

DeLaet, D. L. (2000). *US Immigration Policy in an Age of Rights*. Santa Barbara, CA: Greenwood.

Delgado, R., and Stefancic J. (2001). *Critical Race Theory: An Introduction*. New York, NY: New York University Press.

Deming, D., and Dynarski, S. (2008). "The Lengthening of Childhood." National Bureau of Economic Research (NBER) Working Paper No. 14124.

De Oliveira, M., Santos, M. C., and Kiker, B. F. (2000). "The Role of Human Capital and Technological Change in Over-education." *Economic of Education Review*, 19(2): 199–206.

Deng, F. (2006). "Sudan: A Nation in Turbulent Search for Itself." *Annals of the American Academy of Social and Political Sciences*, 603: 155–162.

Docquier, P., Lohest, O., and Marfouk, A. (2007). "Brain Drain in Developing Countries." *World Bank Economic Review*, 21(2): 193–218.

Dodoo, F. N. (1991). "Earnings Differences among Blacks in America." *Social Science Research*, 20(2): 93–108.

Dodoo, F. N. (1997). "Assimilation Differences among Africans in America." *Social Forces*, 76(2): 527–546.

Dodoo, F. N., and Takyi, B. K. (2002). "Africans in the Diaspora: Black-White Earnings Differences among America's Africans." *Ethnic and Racial Studies*, 25(6): 913–941.

Dolnick, S. (2009). "For African Immigrants, Bronx Culture Clash Turns Violent." *New York Times*, October 19.

Downey, D. B., and Pribesh, S. (2004). "When Race Matters: Teachers' Evaluations of Students' Classroom Behavior." *Sociology of Education*, 77(4): 267–282.

Dreike, O. (2007). "An Investigation into Tourism Certification: A Case Study of the South Luangwa National Park, Zambia." Master's thesis, Durrell Institute of Conservation and Ecology, University of Kent.

Du Bois, W. E. B. (1903). *The Souls of Black Folk*. Chicago, IL: A. C. McClurg.

Dubow, S. (1992). "Africana Nationalism, Apartheid, and the Conceptualization of Race." *Journal of African History*, 33: 209–237.

Duleep, H. O., and Dowhan, D. J. (2008). "Research on Immigrant Earnings." *Social Security Bulletin*, 68(1): 31–50.

Duncan, O.D. (1961). "A socio-economic index for all occupations." In *Occupations and Social Status*, by Albert J. Reiss, Jr., 109–138. New York: The Free Press of Glencoe, Inc.

Duncan, G., and Hoffman, S. D. (1981). "The Incidence and Wage Effects of Overeducation." *Economics of Education Review*, 1(1): 75–86.

Durodoye, B. A., and Coker, A. D. (2008). "Crossing Cultural Marriages: Implications for Counseling African American/African Couples." *International Journal for the Advancement of Counseling*, 30: 25–37.

Eckstein, Z., and Wolpin, K. I. (1999). "Estimating the Effect of Racial Discrimination on First Job Wage Offers." *Review of Economics and Statistics*, 81(3): 384–392.

El-Essawi, D., Musial, J., Hammad, A., and Lim, H. (2007). "A Survey of Skin Disease and Skin-Related Issues in Arab Americans." *Journal of the American Academy of Dermatology*, 56(6): 933–938.

El-Haj, T. R. A. (2006). "Race, Politics, and Arab American Youth: Shifting Frameworks for Conceptualizing Educational Equity." *Educational Policy*, 20(1): 13–34.

El Hamel, C. (2008). "Constructing a Diasporic Identity: Tracing the Origins of the Gnawa Spiritual Group in Morocco." *Journal of African History*, 49(2): 241–260.

El Hamel, C. (2010). "The Register of the Slaves of Sultan Mawlay Isma'il of Morocco at the Turn of the Eighteenth Century." *Journal of African History*, 51, 89–98.

Esipova, N., and Ray, J. (2009). "700 Million Worldwide Desire to Migrate Permanently: US Tops Desired Destination Countries." Gallup, November 2.

Ewans, M. (2002). *European Atrocity, African Catastrophe: Leopold II, the Congo Free State and its Aftermath*. London: RoutledgeCurzon.

Ezza, E. Y., and Libis, A. M. (2010). "The Role of Language in Negotiating Power in the Sudan." *International Journal of African Renaissance Studies*, 5(1): 101–110.

Fabos, A. (2008). "Resisting Blackness: Muslim Arab Sudanese in the Diaspora." *ISM Review*, 21: 24–25.

Fairlie, R. W. (1999). "The Absence of African-American Owned Businesses: An Analysis of the Dynamics of Self-Employment." *Journal of Labor Economics*, 17(1): 80–108.

Fairlie, R. W., and Meyer, B. D. (1996). "Ethnic and Racial Self-Employment Differences and Possible Explanations." *Journal of Human Resources*, 31(4): 757–793.

Findley, H., Fretwell, C., Wheatley, R., and Ingram, E. (2005). "Dressing and Grooming Standards: How Legal Are They?" *Journal of Individual Employment Rights*, 12(2): 165–182.

Fiske, E. B., and Ladd, H. F. (2004). *Elusive Equity: Education Reform in Post-Apartheid South Africa*. Washington, DC: Brookings Institution Press.

Ford, K. (1990). "Duration of Residence in the United States and the Fertility of US Immigrants." *International Migration Review*, 54(1): 34–68.

Forman, T. A., Goar, C., and Lewis, A. E. (2002). "Neither Black nor White? An Empirical Test of the Latin Americanization Thesis." *Race and Society*, 5(1): 65–84.

Frank, R., and Akresh I. (2010). "Latino Immigrants and the US Racial Order: How and Where Do They Fit In?" *American Sociological Review*, 75(3): 378–401.

Freeman, L. (2002). "Does Spatial Assimilation Work for Black Immigrants in the US?" *Urban Studies*, 39(11): 1983–2003.

Frosch, D. (2010). "Immigrants Claim Wal-Mart Fired Them to Provide Jobs for Local Residents." *New York Times*, February 8, 2010.

Fu, V. K. (2001). "Racial Intermarriage Pairings." *Demography*, 38(2): 147–159.

Fu, X., and Heaton, T. B. (2008). "Racial and Educational Homogamy: 1980 to 2000." *Sociological Perspectives*, 51(4): 735–758.

Fuligni, A. J. (1997). "The Academic Achievement of Adolescents from Immigrant Families: The Roles of Family Background, Attitudes, and Behavior." *Child Development*, 68(2): 351–363.

Gee, G. C., and Laflamme, D. F. (2006). "The Association between Self-Reported Discrimination, Physical Health and Blood Pressure: Findings from African Americans, Black Immigrants and Latino Immigrants in New Hampshire." *Journal of Health Care for the Poor and Undeserved*, 17(2): 116–132.

Gold, S. (2004). "From Jim Crow to Racial Hegemony: Evolving Explanations of Racial Hierarchy." *Ethnic and Racial Studies*, 27(6): 952–968.

Gordon, A. (1998). "The New Diaspora: African Immigration to the United States." *Journal of Third World Studies*, 15(1): 79–103.

Gordon, D. F. (1981). "Decolonization and Development in Kenya and Zimbabwe: A Comparative Analysis." *A Journal of Opinion*, 11(3–4): 36–40.

Gordon, E. W., Bridglall, B. L., and Meroe, A. S., eds. (2004). *Supplementary Education: The Hidden Curriculum of High Academic Achievement*. Lanham, MD: Rowman and Littlefield.

Gordon, M. M. (1964). *Assimilation in American Life: The Role of Race, Religion, and National Origins*. New York, NY: Oxford University Press.

Grandmaison, C. (1989). "Rich Cousins, Poor Cousins: Hidden Stratification among Omani Arabs in Eastern Africa." *Africa: Journal of the International African Institute*, 59(2): 176–184.

Grogger, J. (2011). "Speech Patterns and Racial Wage Inequality." *Journal of Human Resources*, 46(1): 1–25.

Gualitieri, S. (2001). "Becoming 'White': Race, Religion and the Foundations of Syrian/Lebanese Ethnicity in the United States." *Journal of American Ethnic History*, 20(4): 29–58.

Hagopian, A., Thompson, M. J., Fordyce, M., Johnson, K. E., and Hart, G. (2004). "The Migration of Physicians from Sub-Saharan Africa to the United States of America: Measures of the African Brain Drain." *Human Resources for Health*, 2: 17.

Hall, M. (2009). "Interstate Migration, Spatial Assimilation, and the Incorporation of US Immigrants." *Population, Space and Place*, 15(1): 57–77.

Hall, M. (2010). "From a World Away to Living Next Door: The Residential Segregation and Attainment of America's Newest Immigrants." PhD dissertation, Pennsylvania State University.

Hammer, J. (2010). "(Almost) Out of Africa: The White Tribes." *World Affairs*, May–June 2010.

Hao, L., and Bonstead-Bruns, M. (1998). "Parent-Child Differences in Educational Expectations and the Academic Achievement of Immigrant and Native Students." *Sociology of Education*, 71(3): 175–198.

Hatton, T. J., and Williamson, J. G. (2003). "Demographic and Economic Pressure on Emigration Out of Africa." *Scandinavian Journal of Economics*, 105(3): 465–486.

Hauser, R. M. (1999). "Should We End Social Promotion? Truth and Consequences." CDE Working Paper No. 99-06, Center for Demography and Ecology, University of Wisconsin–Madison.

Hauser, R. M., Simmons, S. J., and Pager, D. (2000). "High School Dropout, Race-Ethnicity, and Social Background from the 1970s to the 1990s." CDE Working Paper, No. 2000-12, Center for Demography and Ecology, University of Wisconsin–Madison.

Hauser, R. M., and Warren, J. R. (1997). "Socioeconomic Indexes for Occupations: A Review, Update, and Critique." *Sociological Methodology*, 27: 177–298.

Hayes, E. (2009). "African Immigrants Out-Graduate Caucasian Americans and Asians." *Chicago Public Education Examiner*. www.examiner.com/public-education-in-chicago-african-immigrants-out-graduate-american-caucasians-and-asians.

Heaton, T. B., and Jacobson, C. K. (2000). "Intergroup Marriage: An Examination of Opportunity Structures." *Sociological Inquiry*, 70(1): 30–41.

Heisler, B. S. (1992). "The Future of Immigrant Incorporation: Which Models? Which Concepts?" *International Migration Review*, 26(2): 623–641.

Herdin, F., and Nilsson, H. (2009). "The Formalization and Realization Level in Namibian Schools: An Investigation in Two Countryside Schools." Bachelor's thesis in Teacher Education, Linnaeus University.

Herring, C. (2002). "Bleaching Out the Color Line? The Skin Color Continuum and the Tripartite Model of Race." *Race and Society*, 5(1): 17–31.

Hersch, J. (2008). "Profiling the New Immigrant Worker: The Effects of Skin Color and Height." *Journal of Labor Economics*, 26(2): 345–386.

Hirschman, C. (2001). "The Educational Enrollment of Immigrant Youth: A Test of the Segmented Assimilation Hypothesis." *Demography*, 38(3): 317–336.

Hirschman, C., and Wong, M. G. (1984). "Socioeconomic Gains of Asian Americans, Blacks, and Hispanics: 1960–1976." *American Journal of Sociology*, 90(3): 584–607.

Hochschild, J. L., and Cropper, P. (2010). "Immigration Regions and Educational Regimes: Which Countries Promote Rapid Immigrant Incorporation?" *Theory and Research in Education*, 8(21): 21–61.

Hoffmann, T. (2010). "White Kenyan English." In *The Lesser Known Varieties of English*, edited by D. Schreier, P. Trudgill, E. W. Schneider, and J. P. Williams, 286–312. Cambridge: Cambridge University Press.

Hollish, K. (2010). "So Nice to See: Riverside Residents Await Reconstruction." *Twin Cities Daily Planet*. www.tcdailyplanet.net/news/2010/11/03 so-nice-see-riverside-plaza-residents-await-reconstruction.

Huffman, M. L., and Cohen, P. N. (2004). "Racial Wage Inequality: Job Segregation and Devaluation across US Labor Markets." *American Journal of Sociology*, 109(4): 902–936.

Hughes, A. (2006). "African Immigrants to Minnesota Struggle to Gain Ground." Minnesota Public Radio, November 14. http://minnesota.publicradio.org.

Hughes, D. M. (2006). "The Art of Belonging: Whites Writing Landscape in Savanna Africa." Paper presented to the Program in Agrarian Studies, Yale University, New Haven, CT, October 6.

Iceland, J. (2009). *Where We Live Now: Immigration and Race in the United States*. Berkeley: University of California Press.

Jacobs, J. A., and Labov, T. G. (2002). "Gender Differentials in Intermarriage among Sixteen Race and Ethnic Groups." *Sociological Forum*, 17(4): 621–646.

Johnson, S. (2009). "Fleeing from South Africa: Fourteen Years after Apartheid, Why Are the Best and the Brightest Leaving Africa's Most Successful State?" *Newsweek*, February 14.

Jordan, W. (1968). *White over Black: American Attitudes toward the Negro, 1550–1812*. Chapel Hill: University of North Carolina Press.

Journal of Blacks in Higher Education (JBHE). 2000. "African Immigrants in the United States Are the Nation's Most Highly Educated Group." *Journal of Blacks in Higher Education*, 26: 60–61.

Kaba, A. J. (2007). "Educational Attainment, Income Levels and Africans in the United States: The Paradox of Nigerian Immigrants." *West Africa Review*, 11: 1–27.

Kabwe-Segatti, A. W., Landau, L. B., Ellis, S., Vigneswaran, D., and Singh, G. (2006). "Migration in Post-Apartheid South Africa: Challenges and Questions to Policy Makers." *Fonds d'analyse des sociétés politiques*, November 2006.

Kalmijn, M. (1993). "Trends in Black/White Intermarriage." *Social Forces*, 72(1): 119–146.

Kalmijn, M. (1998). "Intermarriage and Homogamy: Causes, Patterns, Trends." *Annual Review of Sociology*, 24: 395–421.

Kamya, H. (2005). "African Immigrant Families." In *Ethnicity and Family Therapy*, edited by M. MacGoldrick, J. Giordano, and N. Garcia Preto, 101–116. 3rd ed. New York, NY: Guilford Press.

Kasirye, G. K. (2008). "Fulani Girls in New York City: Identities, Family and Schooling." PhD. dissertation, Columbia University.

Kaufman, M. (2008). "Eurabia? The Foreign Policy Implications of West Europe's Religious Composition in 2025 and Beyond." Paper presented to the International Studies Association Annual Conference, San Francisco, CA, March 25–29.

Kaushal, N., Kaestner, R., and Reimers, C. (2007). "Labor Market Effects of September 11th on Arab and Muslim Residents of the United States." *Journal of Human Resources*, 42(2), 275–308.

Kawanabe, K. S. (1996). "American Anti-immigrant Rhetoric against Asian Pacific Immigrants: The Present Repeats the Past." *Georgetown Immigration Law Review*, 10: 681–706.

Kayyali, R. A. (2006). *Arab Americans*. Westport, CT: Greenwood Press.

Keita, S. O. Y., and Kittles, A. (1997). "The Persistence of Racial Thinking and the Myth of Racial Divergence." *American Anthropologist*, 99(3): 534–544.

Kent, M. M. (2007). *Immigration and America's Black Population*. Population Bulletin, Vol. 62, No. 4. Washington, DC: Population Reference Bureau.

Kim, C., and Tamborini, R. (2006). "The Continuing Significance of Race in the Occupational Attainment of Whites and Blacks: A Segmented Labor Market Analysis." *Sociological Inquiry*, 76(1): 23–51.

Klasen, S. (1997). "Poverty, Inequality and Deprivation in South Africa: An Analysis of the 1993 SALDRU Survey." *Social Indicators Research*, 41: 51–94.

Kohnert, D. (2007). "African Migration to Europe: Obscured Responsibilities and Common Misconceptions." Working Paper No. 49, Institute of African Affairs at German Institute of Global and Area Studies (GIGA).

Kollehlon, K. T., and Eule, E. E. (2003). "The Socioeconomic Attainment Patterns of Africans in the US." *International Migration Review*, 37(4): 1163–1190.

Konadu-Agyemang, K., and Takyi, B. (2006). "An Overview of African Immigration to the US and Canada." In *The African Diaspora in North Africa: Trends, Community Building, and Adaptation*, edited by K. Konadu-Agyemang, B. Takyi, and J. Arthur, 189–289. Lanham, MD: Lexington Books.

Kroeger, R. A., and Williams, K. (2011). "Consequences of Black Exceptionalism? Interracial Unions with Blacks, Depressive Symptoms, and Relationship Satisfaction." *Sociological Quarterly*, 52(3): 400–420.

Kulczycki, A., and Lobo, A. P. (2002). "Patterns, Implications, and Determinants of Intermarriage among Arab Americans." *Journal of Marriage and the Family*, 64: 202–210.

Laakso, L. (2002). "The Politics of International Election Observation: The Case of Zimbabwe in 2000." *Journal of Modern African Studies*, 40(3): 437–464.

L'Ange, G. (2005). *The White Africans: From Colonization to Liberation*. Jeppestown: Jonathan Ball.

Lee, J. (2009). "Racial Bias Seen in Hiring of Waiters." *New York Times*, March 31. http://cityroom. blogs.nytimes.com/2009/03/31/racial-bias-seen-in-hiring-of-waiters/.

Lee, J., and Bean, F. (2004). "America's Changing Color Lines: Immigration, Race/Ethnicity, and Multiracial Identification." *Annual Review of Sociology*, 30: 221–242.

Lee, J., and Bean, F. (2007). "Redrawing the Color Line?" *City and Community*, 6(1): 49–62.

Lee, J., and Bean F. (2010). *The Diversity Paradox: Immigration and the Color line in 21st-Century America*. New York, NY: Russell Sage Foundation.

Lee, S. M. (1989). "Asian Immigration and American Race-Relations: From Exclusion to Acceptance?" *Racial and Ethnic Studies*, 12(3): 368–390.

Lee, S. M., and Edmonston, B. (2005). "New Marriages, New Families: US Racial and Hispanic Intermarriage." *Population Bulletin*, 60(2): 3–36.

Leicht, K. T. (2008). "Broken Down by Race and Gender? Sociological Explanations of New Sources of Earnings Inequality." *Annual Review of Sociology*, 34: 237–255.

Lichter, D. T., LeClere, F. B., and McLaughlin, D. K. (1991). "Local Marriage Markets and the Marital Behavior of Black and White Women." *American Journal of Sociology*, 96(4): 843–867.

Lichter, D. T., McLaughlin, D. K., Kephart, G., and Landry, D. J. (1992). "Race and the Retreat from Marriage: A Shortage of Marriageable Men?" *American Sociological Review*, 57(6): 781–799.

Lieberson, S. (1961). "A Societal Theory of Race and Ethnic Relations." *American Sociological Review*, 26(6): 902–910.

Lieberson, S. (1981). *A Piece of the Pie: Black and White Immigrants since 1880*. Berkeley: University of California Press.

Lobo, A. (2001). "US Diversity Visas Are Attracting Africa's Best and Brightest." *Population Today*, 29(5): 1–2.

Lobo, A. (2006). "Unintended consequences: Liberalized US Immigration Law and the African Brain Drain." In *The African Diaspora in North Africa: Trends, Community Building, and Adaptation*, edited by K. Konadu-Agyemang, B. Takyi, and J. Arthur, 189–289. Lanham, MD, Lexington Books.

Lofstrom, M. (2000). "Self-Employment and Earning among Highly Skilled Immigrants in the United States." IZA Discussion Paper No. 175.

Logan, J. R., and Deane, G. (2003). "Black Diversity in Metropolitan America." Lewis Mumford Center for Comparative Urban and Regional Research, University of Albany.

Lucassen, L., and Laarman, C. (2009). "Immigration, Intermarriage and the Changing Face of Europe in the Post War Period." *History of the Family*, 14: 52–68.

Marrow, H. B. (2009). "New Immigrant Destinations and the American Color Line." *Ethnic and Racial Studies*, 32(6): 1037–1057.

Martinez, G. A. (2006). "Immigration and the Meaning of United States Citizenship: Whiteness and Assimilation." *Washburn Law Journal*, 46(1): 335–344.

Massey, D. S. (1990). "The Social and Economic Origins of Immigration." *Annals of the American Academy of Political and Social Science*, 510: 60–70.

Massey, D. S., Arango, J., Hugo, G., Kouaouci, A., Pellegrino, A., and Taylor, J. E. (1998). *Worlds in Motion: Understanding International Migration at the End of the Millennium*. New York, NY: Oxford University Press.

Mattoo, A., Neagu, I. C., and Ozden, C. (2008). "Brain Waste? Educated Immigrants in the US Labor Market." *Journal of Development Economics*, 87: 255–269.

Maxim, P. S. (1992). "Immigrants, Visible Minorities, and Self-Employment." *Demography*, 29(2): 181–198.

Mazuri, A. (1964). "Political Sex." *Transition*, 17: 19–23.

Mazuri, A. (1973). "The Black Arabs in Comparative Perspective." In *The Southern Sudan and the Problem of Integration*, edited by D. M. Wai, 47–82. London: Frank Cass.

Mbaya, M., Mrina, P., and Levin, M. (2007). "What the 2000 US Census Tells Us about the Kenyan Diaspora." *Journal of Global Initiatives: Policy, Pedagogy, Perspective*, 2(2): 130–150.

McAdoo, H. P., Younge, S., and Getahun, S. (2007). "Marriage and Family Socialization among Black Americans and Caribbean and African Immigrants." In *The Other African Americans*, edited by Y. Shaw-Taylor and S. A. Tuch, 93–166. Lanham, MD: Rowman and Littlefield.

McDermott, M., and Samson, F. L. (2004). "White Racial and Ethnic Identity in the United States." *Annual Review of Sociology*, 31: 245–261.

Meng, X., and Gregory, R. G. (2005). "Intermarriage and the Economic Assimilation of Immigrants." *Journal of Labor Economics*, 23(1): 135–176.

Merton, R. K. (1941). "Intermarriage and the Social Structure: Fact and Theory." *Psychiatry*, 4: 361–374.

Middleton, N., and O'Keefe, P. (2006). "Politics, History, and Problems of Humanitarian Assistance in Sudan." *Review of African Political Economy*, 33(109): 543–559.

Miech, R. A., Eaton, W., and Liang, K. (2003). "Occupational Stratification over the Life Course: A Comparison of Occupational Trajectories across Race and Gender during the 1980s and 1990s." *Work and Occupations*, 30(4): 440–473.

Model, S. (1991). "Caribbean Immigrants: A Black Success Story?" *International Migration Review*, 25(2): 248–276.

Model, S. (1995). "West Indian Prosperity: Fact or Fiction?" *Social Problems*, 42(4): 535–553.

Model, S. (1997). "An Occupational Tale of Two Cities: Minorities in London and New York." *Demography*, 34(4): 539–550.

Model, S. (2008). *West Indian Immigrants: A Black Success Story?* Russell Sage Foundation Publications.

Moore, A. R., and Amey, F. K. (2002). "Earnings Differentials among Male African Immigrants in the United States." *Equal Opportunities International*, 21(8): 30–50.

Morse, D. (2009). "The US African Consumer Segment." Paper presented to the Fifth Annual Multicultural Midwest Conference, April 26.

Moss, P. I., and Tilly, C. (1995). "Skills and Race in Hiring: Quantitative Findings from Face-to-Face Interviews." *Eastern Economic Journal*, 21(3): 357–374.

Moss, P. I., and Tilly, C. (2003). *Stories Employers Tell: Race, Skill, and Hiring in America*. New York, NY: Russell Sage Foundation.

Mpofu, E., Thomas, K. R., and Chan, F. (2004). "Social Competence in Zimbabwean Multicultural Schools: Effects of Ethnic and Gender Differences." *International Journal of Psychology*, 39(3): 169–178.

Mpofu, E., and Watkins, D. (1997). "Self-Concept and Social Acceptance in Multiracial African Schools: A Test of Insulation, Subjective Culture, and Bicultural Competence Hypothesis." *Cross-Cultural Research*, 31(4): 331–355.

Mrad-Dali, I. (2005). "De l'esclavage à la servitude: Le cas des Noirs de Tunisie." *Cahiers d'Études africaines*, December 21. http://etudesafricaines.revues.org/5704.

Mrad-Dali, I. (2010). "Identités multiples et multitudes d'histoires: Les 'Noirs tunisiens' de 1846 à aujourd' hui." *L'Atelier du Centre de Recherches Historiques, Revue électronique du CRH*, May 7. http://etudesafricaines.revues.org/5704.

Murphy, J. (2004). "Mozambique's Daughter: Present-day Africa No Longer Matches Teresa Heinz Kerry's Memories of Her Childhood There." *Baltimore Sun*, February 24. http://www.baltimoresun.com/news/bal-teresa0224,0,7071724.story?page=1.

Murguia, E., and Telles, E. (1996). "Phenotype and Schooling among Mexican Americans." *Sociology of Education*, 69(4): 276–289.

Musvoto, A. R. (2009). "Filling the Void in Our National Life: The Search for a Song That Captures the Spirit of Rhodesian Nationalism and National Identity." *Muziki*, 6(2): 154–162.

Mutua, M. (2000). "Critical Race Theory and International Law: The View of an Insider-Outsider Symposium." *Villanova Law Review*, 45: 841–854.

Naber, N. (2000). "Ambiguous Insiders: An Investigation of Arab American Invisibility." *Ethnic and Racial Studies*, 23(1): 37–61.

Naber, N. (2005). "Muslim First, Arab Second: A Strategic Politics of Race and Gender." *Muslim World*, 95: 479–495.

Naber, N. (2008). "Introduction." In *Race and Arab Americans Before and African 9/11: From Invisible Citizens to Visible Subjects*, edited by A. Jamal and N. Naber, 1–45. Syracuse, NY: Syracuse University Press.

Newton, A. A. (2005). "Injecting Diversity into US Immigration Policy: The Diversity Visa Program and the Missing Discourse on African Immigration to the United States." *Cornell International Law Journal*, 38: 1049–1078.

Ngai, M. M. (2009). "The Johnson-Reed Act of 1924 and the Reconstruction of Race in Immigration Law." In *American Studies: An Anthology*, edited by J. A. Radway, K. K. Gaines, B. Shank, and P. Von Eschen, 69–77. Hoboken, NJ: Willey-Blackwell.

Nigem, E. T. (1986). "Arab Americans: Migration, Socioeconomic and Demographic Characteristics." *International Migration Review*, 20(3): 629–649.

Njue, J., and Retish, P. (2010). "Transitioning: Academic and Social Performance of African Students in an American High School." *Urban Education*, 45(3): 347–370.

Noel, D. L. (1968). "A Theory of the Origin of Ethnic Stratification." *Social Problems*, 16(2): 157–172.

Nyamweru, C. (2001). "Letting the Side Down: Personal Reflections on Colonial and Independent Kenya." In *Global Multiculturalism: Comparative Perspectives on Race, Ethnicity, and Nation*, edited by H. H. Corwell and E.W. Stoddard, 169–192. Lanham, MD: Rowman and Littlefield.

Ogbu, J. U. (1987). "Variability in Minority School Performance: A Problem in Search of an Explanation." *Anthropology & Education Quarterly*, 18(4): 312–334.

Oliver, M. L., and Shapiro, T. M. (2006). *Black Wealth, White Wealth: A New Perspective on Racial Inequality*. New York, NY: Routledge.

Omi, M., and Winant, H. (1994). *Racial Formation in the United States: From the 1960s to the 1990s*. 2nd ed. New York, NY: Routledge.

Orieny, P. O. (2008). "African Immigrants' Stressful Marital and Family Experiences." PhD dissertation, University of Minnesota.

Osada, M. (2002). *Sanctions and Honorary Whites: Diplomatic Policies and Economic Realities in Relations between Japan and South Africa*. Santa Barbara, CA: Greenwood Press.

Osborne, A. H., Vance, D., Rohling, E. J., Barton, N., Rogerson, M., and Fello, N. (2008). "A Humid Corridor across the Sahara for the Migration of Early Modern Humans Out of Africa 120,000 Years Ago." *Proceedings of the National Academy of Sciences*, 105(43): 16444–16447.

O'Toole, T. (2007). "The Historical Context." In *Understanding Contemporary Africa*, edited by A. A. Gordon and D. L. Gordon, 23–56. 4th ed. Boulder, CO: Lyne Reinner.

Page, C. (2007). "Black Immigrant Model Minorities." Far Outliers, March. http://faroutliers.wordpress.com/2007/03/19/black-immigrant-model-minorities/.

Pagnini, D. L., and Morgan, S. P. (1990). "Intermarriage and Social Distance among US Immigrants at the Turn of the Century." *American Journal of Sociology*, 96(2): 405–432.

Parisi, D., Lichter, D. T., and Taquino, M. C. (2011). "Multi-scale Residential Segregation: Black Exceptionalism and America's Changing Color Line." *Social Forces*, 89(3): 829–852.

Perry, D. L. (1997). "Rural Ideologies and Urban Imaginings: Wolof Immigrants in New York City." *Africa Today*, 44(2): 229–259.

Pickett, M. F., and Pickett, D. W. (2011). *The European Struggle to Settle North America: Colonizing Attempts by England, France and Spain, 1521–1608*. Jefferson, NC: McFarland.

Pierre, J. (2004). "Black Immigrants in the United States and the Cultural Narratives of Ethnicity." *Identities: Global Studies in Culture and Power*, 11: 141–170.

Portes, A., and Borocz, J. (1989). "Contemporary Immigration: Theoretical Perspectives and Modes of Incorporation." *International Migration Review*, 23(3): 606–630.

Portes, A., and Zhou, M. (1992). "Divergent Destinies: Immigration, Poverty and Entrepreneurship." Joint Center for Political and Economic Studies, Washington, DC.

Portes, A., and Zhou, M. (1993). "The New Second Generation: Segmented Assimilation and Its Variants." *Annals of the American Academy of Political and Social Science*, 30: 74–96.

Portes, A., and Zhou, M. (1996). "Self-Employment and the Earnings of Immigrants." *American Sociological Review*, 61(2): 219–230.

Power, D. V., and Shandy, D. J. (1998). "Sudanese Refugees in a Minnesota Family Practice Clinic." *Family Medicine*, 30(3): 185–189.

Power, J. (1993). "Race, Class, Ethnicity, and Anglo-Indian Trade Rivalry in Colonial Malawi, 1910–1945." *International Journal of African Historical Studies*, 26(3): 575–607.

Qian, Z., and Lichter, D. T. (2001). "Measuring Marital Assimilation: Intermarriage among Natives and Immigrants." *Social Science Research*, 30(2): 289–312.

Qian, Z., and Lichter, D. T. (2007). "Social boundaries and marital assimilation: Interpreting trends in racial and ethnic intermarriage." *American Sociological Review*, 72(1), 68–94.

Quinn, M. A., and Rubb, S. (2005). "Education-Occupation Matching in Migration Decisions." *Demography*, 42(1): 153–167.

Quintana-Murci, L., Semino, O., Bandelt, H., Passarino, G., McElreavey, K., and Santachiara-Benerecetti, A. (1999). "Genetic Evidence of an Early Exit of Homo Sapiens from Africa through Eastern Africa." *Nature Genetics*, 23: 437–441.

Read, J. G. (2003). "The Sources of Gender Role Attitudes among Christian and Muslim Arab-American Women." *Sociology of Religion*, 64(2): 207–222.

Read, J. G. (2004). "Cultural Influences on Immigrant Women's Labor Force Participation: The Arab-American Case." *International Migration Review*, 38(1): 52–77.

Reiter, B. (2010). "Immigrants Find Old Careers Don't Transfer to New Life." *Kansas City Star*, May 14, 2010.

Reitz, J. G. (2001). "Immigrant Skill Utilization in the Canadian Labour Market: Implications of Human Capital Research." *Journal of International Migration and Integration*, 2(6): 347–378.

Reitz, J. G., and Sklar, S. M. (1997). "Culture, Race, and the Economic Assimilation of Immigrants." *Sociological Forum*, 12(2): 233–277.

Reynolds, R. R. (2002). "An African Brain Drain: Igbo Decisions to Immigrate to the US." *Review of African Political Economy*, 29(92): 273–284.

Rimer, S., and Arenson, K. W. (2004). "Top Colleges Take More Blacks, but Which Ones?" *New York Times*, June 24.

Roberts, S. (2005). "More Africans Enter U.S. Than in Days of Slavery," *New York Times*, February 21, 2005, http://mumford.albany.edu/census/othersay/02212005NewYorkTimes.pdf.

Rockquemore, K., and Arend, P. (2002). "Opting for White: Choice, Fluidity, and Racial Identity Formation in Post Civil-Rights America." *Race and Society*, 5(1): 49–64.

Rong, X. L., and Brown, F. (2001). "The Effects of Immigrant Generation and Ethnicity on Educational Attainment among Young African and Caribbean Immigrants in the United States." *Harvard Educational Review*, 71(3): 536–565.

Rosen, A. B., Tsai, J. S., and Downs, S. P. (2003). "Variations in Risk Attitude across Race, Gender, and Education." *Medical Decision Making*, 23: 511.

Rosenfeld, M. J. (2002). "Measure of Assimilation in the Marriage Market: Mexican Americans 1970 to 1990." *Journal of Marriage and the Family*, 64(1): 152–162.

Rumbaut, R. G. (1994). "Origins and Destinies: Immigration to the United States since World War II." *Sociological Forum*, 9(4): 583–621.

Salt, J. (2005). *Current Trends in International Migration in Europe*. Strasbourg: Council of Europe.

Sanchez, G. J. (1997). "Face the Nation: Race, Immigration, and the Rise of Nativism in Late Twentieth Century America." *International Migration Review*, 31(4): 1009–1030.

Sanders, J. M., and Nee, V. (1996). "Immigrant Self-Employment: The Family as Social Capital and the Value of Human Capital." *American Sociological Review*, 61(2): 231–249.

Sassler, S. (2005). "Gender and Ethnic Differences in Marital Assimilation in the Early Twentieth Century." *International Migration Review*, 39(3): 608–636.

Satterfield, T. A., Mertz, C. K., and Slovic, P. (2004). "Discrimination, Vulnerability, and Justice in the Face of Risk." *Risk Analysis*, 24(1): 115–129.

Schultz, T. P. (1998). "Immigrant Quality and Assimilation: A Review of the US Literature." *Journal of Population Economics*, 11(2): 239–252.

Sears, D. O., Fu, M., Henry, P., and Bui, K. (2003). "The Origins and Persistence of Ethnic Identity among 'New Immigrant' Groups." *Social Psychology Quarterly*, 66(4): 419–437.

Sears, D. O., and Savalei, V. (2006). "The Political Color Line in America: Many 'Peoples of Color' or Black Exceptionalism?" *Political Psychology*, 27(6): 895–924.

Segal, R. (2002). *Islam's Black Slaves: The Other Black Diaspora*. New York, NY: Farrar, Strauss and Giroux.

Seligman, C. G. (1966). *Races of Africa*. New York, NY: Oxford University Press.

Shamhan, H. H. (2001). "Who Are Arab Americans?" *Grolier's Multimedia Encyclopedia*.

Sharkey, H. J. (2007). "Arab Identity and Ideology in Sudan: The Politics of Language Ethnicity and Race." *African Affairs*, 107(426): 21–43.

Shryock, A. (2010). "Introduction: Islam as an Object of Fear and Affection." In *Islamophobia/Islamophilia: Beyond the Politics of Enemy and Friend*, edited by A. Shryock, 1–28. Bloomington: Indiana University Press.

Silverman, S. M. (2004). "Theron Finally Cries over Oscar Win." *People*, March 11.

Sirtima, I. V., ed. (2009). *The Golden Age of Moor*. Piscataway, NJ: Transaction Publishers.

Skrentny, J. D. (2001). "Affirmative Action and New Demographic Realities." http://chronicle.com/article/Affirmative-ActionNew/13634.

Smith, K. R., Zick, C. D., and Duncan, G. J. (1991). "Remarriage Patterns among Recent Widows and Widowers." *Demography*, 28(3): 361–374.

Spear, T. (1994). "The Newest African Americans Aren't Black." *American Demographics*, 16(1): 9–10.

Stewart, Q., and Dixon, J. C. (2010). "Is It Race, Immigrant Status, or Both: An Analysis of Wage Disparities among Immigrant Men in the US." *International Migration Review*, 44(1): 173–201.

Stoller, P. (2001). "West Africans: Trading Places in New York." In *New Immigrants in New York*, edited by N. Foner, 229–250. New York, NY: Columbia University Press.

Stoller, P. (2002). *Money Has No Smell: The Africanization of New York City*. Chicago, IL: University of Chicago Press.

Sue, C. (2009). "An Assessment of the Latin Americanization Thesis." *Ethnic and Racial Studies*, 32(6): 1058–1070.

Takyi, B. K., and Konadu-Agyemang, K. (2006). "Theoretical Perspectives on African Immigration." In *The New African Diaspora in North America*, edited by B. K. Takyi and K. Konadu-Agyemang, 13–28. Lanham, MD: Rowman and Littlefield.

Telles, E. E., and Murguia, E. (1990). "Phenotypic Discrimination and Income Differences among Mexican-Americans." *Social Science Quarterly*, 71(4): 682–696.

Terrazas, A. (2009). "African Immigrants in the United States." *Migration Information Source*, February.

Thomas, K. J. A. (2009). "Parental Characteristics and the Schooling Progress of Black Immigrant and Native-Born Children." *Demography*, 46(3): 513–534.

Thomas, K. J. A. (2010). "Household Context, Generational Status, and English Proficiency Among the Children of African Immigrants in the United States," *International Migration Review*, 44(1): 142–172.

Thomas, K. J. A. (2011a). "What Explains the Increasing Trend in African Emigration to the US?" *International Migration Review*, 45(1): 3–28.

Thomas, K. J. A. (2011b). "Familial Influences on Child Poverty in Black Immigrant, US-Born Black, and Non-Black Immigrant Families." *Demography*, 48(2): 437–460.

Thomas, K. J. A. (2012). "Race and Enrollment Disparities among the Children of Immigrants: An Examination of Differences between the Children of Black and White Africans." *International Migration Review*, 46(1): 37–60

Tienda, M. (2011). "Hispanics and US Schools: Problems, Puzzles, and Possibilities." *Frontiers in Sociology and Social Research*, 1(2): 303–310.

Tolnay, S. E. (2001). "African Americans and Immigrants in Northern Cities: The Effects of Relative Group Size on Occupational Standing in 1920." *Social Forces*, 80(2): 573–604.

Turner, J. H. (1986). "Toward a Unified Theory of Ethnic Antagonism: A Preliminary Synthesis of Three Macro Models." *Sociological Forum*, 1(3): 403–427.

Vaisey, S. (2006). "Education and Its Discontents: Overqualification in America, 1972–2002." *Social Forces*, 85: 835–864.

van Tubergen, F., and Maas, I. (2007). "Ethnic Intermarriage among Immigrants in the Netherlands: An Analysis of Population Data." *Social Science Research*, 36: 1065–1086.

Vaughn, L. M., and Holloway, M. (2010). "West African Immigrant Families from Mauritania and Senegal in Cincinnati: A Cultural Primer." *Journal of Community Health*, 35: 27–35.

Washington, R. E. (1990). "Brown Racism and the Formation of a World System of Racial Stratification." *International Journal of Politics, Culture, and Society*, 4(2): 209–227.

Waters, M. C. (1999). *Black Identities: West Indian Immigrant Dreams and American Realities*. Cambridge, MA: Harvard University Press.

Waters, M. C., and Eschbach, K. (1995). "Immigration and Ethnic and Racial Inequality in the United States." *Annual Review of Sociology*, 21: 419–446.

Waters, M. C., and Jimenez, T. R. (2005). "Assessing Immigrant Assimilation: New Empirical and Theoretical Challenges." Annual Review of Sociology, 31: 105–125.

West, R. (1965). *The White Tribes of Africa*. New York, NY: Macmillan.

Wilson, C. A. (1996). *Racism: From Slavery to Advanced Capitalism*. Thousand Oaks, CA: Sage.

Wilson, J. H. (2008). "African-Born Blacks in the Washington, D.C., Metro Area." Population Reference Bureau.

Wilson, J. H., and Habecker, S. (2008). "The Lure of the Capital City: An Anthro-Geographical Analysis of Recent African Immigration to Washington, D.C." *Population, Space, and Place*, 14: 433–448.

Wingfield, M. (2006). "Arab Americans: Into the Multicultural Mainstream." *Equity & Excellence in Education*, 39(3): 253–266.

World Bank. (2010). *World Development Indicators 2009*. Washington, DC: World Bank.

Xie, Y., and Goyette, K. (2003). "Social Mobility and the Educational Choices of Asian Americans." *Social Science Research*, 32(3): 467–498.

Yancey, G. (2003). *Who Is White? Latinos, Asians, and the New Black/Nonblack Divide*. Boulder, CO: Lynne Reiner.

Yancey, G. (2009). "Cross Racial Differences in the Racial Preferences of Potential Dating Partners: A Test of the Alienation of African Americans and Social Dominance Orientation." *Sociological Quarterly*, 50: 121–134.

Zavodny, M. (2003). "Race, Wages, and Assimilation among Cubans." *Population Research and Policy Review*, 22: 201–219.

Zhou, M. (1997). "Segmented Assimilation: Issues, Controversies, and Recent Research on the New Second Generation." *International Migration Review*, 31(4): 955–1008.

Zlotnik, H. (1998). "International Migration: 1965–96: An Overview." *Population and Development Studies*, 24(3): 429–468.

Zolberg, A. R. (1999). "Matters of State: Theorizing Immigration Policy." In *The Handbook of International Migration: The American Experience*, edited by C. Hirschman, P. Kasinitz, and J. DeWind, 71–93. New York, NY: Russell Sage Foundation.

Index